IN PLAIN SIGHT

THE DISREGARDED TRUTH

The only difference between the *United States of America* today and that of other socialist and communist countries is the illusion of unity, liberty, and freedom!

> "It is wrong for the governments of our country to believe that they can place regulatory limitations upon the rights, liberties, and freedoms that the American people possess and then act upon their beliefs by accusing the American people of committing victimless crimes and then immorally punishing them for such. To do so is a criminal act in and of itself." P. McConkey

Written By: Paul McConkey

Published by:

Createspace.com an Amazon.com Company

To order additional copies of this book go www.amazon.com

Library of Congress Cataloging-in-Publication Data

Not available at the time of publication

ISBN-13: 978-1460963012

ISBN-10: 1460963016

20111014-2305A

Special Thanks

"There is no difference between the people in Washington D.C. and the people in Hollywood, they're the actors and we're the audience."

Karen M.

"Look out Harry Houdini, and all magicians of the world, the leaders of our great country have performed the grandest magic trick seen by all of mankind, while perfecting the art of slight of hand on the American people."

Bryant H.

"How do you morally and ethically obey tax laws that are not respected nor obeyed by the self-same people that were elected and appointed to enforce the tax laws? Government officials and its employees should never be allowed to tell the American people; do what I say and not what I do."

Colvin B.

I have to extend a special thanks to each person listed above, for his and her assistance and continued support.

Thank you Bryant, thank you Colvin, and, more importantly, thank you Karen.

"All truths are easy to understand once they are discovered; the point is to discover them."

Galileo Galilei

"Freedom is never more than one generation away from extinction. We didn't pass it to our children in the bloodstream. It must be fought for, protected, and handed on for them to do the same."

Ronald Reagan

"All tyranny needs to gain a foothold is for people of good conscience to remain silent."

Thomas Jefferson

Table of Contents

"Most people spend more time and energy going around problems than in trying to solve them."

Henry Ford

"Sometimes it is said that man cannot be trusted with the government of himself. Can he, then be trusted with the government of others? Or have we found angels in the form of kings to govern him? Let history answer this question."

Thomas Jefferson

About the Author:

As a child that grew up just outside Washington D.C., during the 1970's and 80's, I noted several contradictions and inconsistencies with the rules of our society. More importantly, I started to see a hypocrisy that was trying to trump the American way of life. My siblings, parents, and friends had always said that I was making too much out of what I was noticing and they assured me the American way of life was secure. They also added that our government officials would never break the Law nor would German Gestapo like tactics ever again be practice, especially here in America. To my disbelief, I was introduced to even more lies and acts of betrayal when I a Marine in the United States Marine Corps, a Law Enforcement Officer within the Department of Corrections, and within a Sheriff's Department. As I became exposed to the inner workings of the Federal, State, and local governments, I noticed a double standard that was illegally and unjustly being imposed on the American people. Because of the unlawful actions taken by "our" government, I resorted to studying the Law. The areas in which my studies directed me into consisted of; Administrative Law, Contract Law, Real Estate Law, Common Law, and Constitutional Law. The key to understanding any given Law is to know were its authority originates from. Due to the fact the American people are lacking the knowledge on how to determine the authority of any given Law, the governments of our country have been misapplying certain Laws. The unlawful actions taken by those employed by government violate the oath that I swore to when I stated that I would support and defend the Constitution of the United States against all enemies, foreign and domestic. Therefore, I feel compelled to bring fourth the truth with the hope that we, the American people, will once again reunite and return our country to the beloved land of the free. To their disbelief, the American people are now seeing German Gestapo like tactics which have revealed their ugly heads once again; however, this is occurring not in a faraway land but rather here in America!

"Truth is a deep kindness that teaches us to be content in our everyday life and share with people the same happiness."

Kahlil Gibran

"The ultimate measure of a man is not where he stands in moments of comfort and convenience, but where he stands at times of challenge and controversy."

Dr. Martin Luther King, Jr.

"Our federal tax system is, in short, utterly impossible, utterly unjust, and completely counterproductive, it reeks with injustice and is fundamentally un-American . . . It has earned a rebellion and it's time we rebelled."

Ronald Reagan

Words of Encouragement

Over the past 25 years, while in the military, law enforcement, and during my studies of Law, I have recognized that one aspect of the American way of life stands out above the rest. **It is wrong for the governments of our country to place regulatory limitations on the rights, liberties, and freedoms of the American people and then immorally punishing them by accusing innocent people of committing victimless crimes. To do so is a criminal act in itself.** Therefore, the people are not criminals for merely wanting to exist or because they have decided to exercise anyone of their rights, liberties, or freedoms. On the contrary, the criminals here consist of those that have found their way into a government position and have forcibly taken action and have began an attack on the American people, by using the force of government itself. This is especially true when an innocent person has not in any way harmed another human being. With that said, we need to recognize the truth and correct the injustices that are occurring. We, the American people, have always held the authority to charge and punish the individuals that have committed crimes, even though they may be a government official or employee. However, we as a society have either forgotten or we were never taught the correct process in which we should handle these matters. This book will help those that are interested in correcting the injustices and punishing those that have broken their oath to protect the American people. One person cannot do it alone. However, as a whole, The People will prevail.

"All, too, will bear in mind this sacred principle, that though the will of the majority is in all cases to prevail, that will to be rightful must be reasonable; that the minority possess their equal rights, which equal law must protect, and to violate would be oppression."

Thomas Jefferson

"You're not supposed to be so blind with patriotism that you can't face reality. Wrong is wrong no matter who does it or says it."

Malcolm X

Remember This Quote, It's Important

"You can never have a revolution in order to establish a Democracy. You must have a Democracy in order to have a revolution."

Gilbert K. Chesterton

Introduction
The Truth Begins Here

"It isn't that they can't see the solution. It is that they can't see the problem." *Gilbert K. Chesterton*

Please be aware that some of the topics discussed in this book are, to some people, forbidden in nature. Why, I have no idea. Even so, you will learn about the developments that have been taking place over the past 97 years that have been robbing us of our wealth and, more importantly, our rights, liberties, and freedoms. Along the way, you will discover many fascinating and disturbing facts about our way of life. Even though the United States of America was the world's industrial leader, during the 19th century, and the wealthiest, freest, and most prosperous country, during the beginning part of the 20th century, something horrible was about to occur. It would be the most horrific change that would ever occur to a free America. It all took place because of the fact the American people were too divided and morally decrepit to stop it. Today, most of the American population has allowed their laziness and complacency to cloud their judgment. This especially applies when it concerns the founding principles of our free America and what its supposed to be. Most of the American people are allowing the original intent of our country to continue down a journey to a state of nonexistence. The freedoms, rights, and liberties once enjoyed by the American people, who grew up during the 18th, 19th, and early part of the 20th century, will soon cease to exist. To make matters worse, most of the American people do not care to know that our rights, liberties, and freedoms are being destroyed. It is appalling to see that when I engage myself in a conversation with an uninformed individual that these topics somehow become forbidden in nature. In addition, it also seems like the governments of our country believe that we, as free Americans, shouldn't mention these issues. Are we living in Germany with the fear that Hitler's Gestapo will hear us talking about the issues of government and will punish us for doing so? Yes, this is happening in America today!

Still, these issues are too important to ignore any longer. You may have asked yourself one or two of the same questions, but may not have been able to put the complete picture together. With the hope that this book will reach the mass majority of the American people, I have written it in simple terms. I have found that this is the best way to reach most of my fellow Americans and; I hope, it will allow me to explain my findings. Occasionally, I may have to use terminology that may confuse some people; however, this is because the governments of our country have created their own secret language. Nonetheless, I will make it as simple as possible. The goal of this book is to open the eyes of the American people by revealing the truth of how the American way of life has changed over the years. I can no longer stand for the lies, deceptions, and the dishonesty that our government is committing against the American people. The perpetrators consist of certain socialistic individuals that have found their way into the banking industry and into the government itself. The American people should never tolerate a socialistic attitude or behavior within our free society. Why? For if a free people were to ignore this behavior, they will find themselves waking up one morning in an unfair, unjust, and communistic country ruled by a few self-proclaimed individuals.

Even though a form of socialism and communistic behavior has surfaced here in America, why is it that good hardworking Americans just stand by and allow these socialistic individuals, which have found their way into a government position, to have the ability to take away their wealth, rights, and liberties, while ignoring and breaking the law itself? I could have never imagined the American people would be so weak as to allow the governments of our country to violate the law, break the confines of the Constitution, and trample into their everyday lives. This is being accomplished by a systematic use of lies and deceptions. The sad part is the American people know the government is lying to them, but yet they do nothing. Therefore, it is my hope that you'll find this book enlightening and, more importantly, that it will help you to understand the truth about what's happening to our beloved country. At some point, you may have wanted to talk about these issues, but just like most of your fellow Americans you felt that these topics were too controversial. In return, you kept your mouth shut because you were worried that your friends and acquaintances would see you as being un-American. If this is the case, I don't want you to worry. If you are concerned about your rights and liberties disappearing you can never be seen as un-American. It doesn't take an expert to see something for what it is, that's if your eyes and mind are open to the truth. Use your common sense and you'll have no problem with understanding the issues. The key is to keep an open mind and you will see the truth. I have written this book with the belief that if most of the American people were to be made aware of the lies, inconsistencies, and contradictions that have been designed to rob us of our rights, liberties, and wealth that we will once again stand together to make a change, just like the founding fathers did. Still, I am amazed to hear that most of the American people are too afraid to do anything to correct the injustices. It is difficult for me to believe that we, the American people, are no longer living in the country nicknamed the "Home of the Brave". The reason we are facing an out of control government and an economy that borders a catastrophic collapse is because of the overall ignorance of the law and that of the underlying principles of our free America. This includes keeping the government within its original intent by using the law set forth by the passage of the Constitution. At this point, I must ask you an important question. Have you ever been in a courtroom? If not, this only means that you have not had the chance to experience an injustice from a government entity or have not had the pleasure of a government agency turning your life upside down, at least not yet. Even so, I still believe that you, as an American, will take a stand no matter the circumstances. Therefore, if an injustice were to occur, I choose to believe the majority of the American people will once again reunite with one another, confront the persons that have committed the criminal act, and help correct the injustice, even if the criminal act were to be perpetrated by a government entity. Why do I believe this? I believe this for one main reason, if an unjust law had been passed, without any thought of its ramifications, it could be used against you or your family. I understand that it all depends on where you're line has been drawn and if anyone has crossed it or not. With that said, there is a simple solution to avoiding any violation that may occur to someone's rights and liberties. All you have to do, that's if you're in a position of authority, would be to ask yourself one question. How would you feel if an unjust law was used against you? One of the main problems that I am seeing today is that there are laws are being passed without any consideration as to their constitutionality or if they are morally correct or not. For the most part, claims are being made to laws that do not exist. The governments of our country, along with their officials, are making them up as they go along and have chosen to blindly follow hearsay. Furthermore, you cannot legislate morality with immoral laws and enforce them with an immoral behavior. When we depart from using civility and turn to a false sense of security by using force, with good intentions or otherwise, the immoral value inherently associated with the use of force will always prevail over good intentions. Still, it may be difficult for some people to embrace these issues and/or concerns. However, it is imperative that we at least ask ourselves are these worth bringing up? I believe they are.

During my everyday interaction with my friends, acquaintances, and co-workers these issues have come up from time to time. In the past, I have had to sidestep many issues concerning our rights, liberties, and freedoms, which includes avoiding issues that concern the actions taken by our government. At times, this can be upsetting because we, as fellow Americans, cannot discuss these matters. Some people, confusingly enough, refuse to hear anything negative about "their" government and what is taking place in America today. They remind me of the "See No Evil", "Hear No Evil", "Speak No Evil" monkeys. However, some of the people that I have encountered have asked me, "Why are you so passionate about these issues?" I respond with, I'm tired of all the lies. I have been lied to all my life about important issues concerning our rights, liberties, and the authority and proper role of the government. Therefore, I will not stand for any more lies. In addition, if seeking the truth and having the will to make a change is wrong, then I want to be wrong. I will die for what I stand for; however, most of the American population will not stand up for their beliefs. That's if they have any beliefs to begin with. The majority of the American population's primary focus is on celebrities, watching reality shows, and engulfing themselves with material objects. Most people have no interest in watching the government or correcting the unlawful acts the government has engaged itself in. What's even more confusing is that most of the American people, including those within government, have no interest in protecting their own rights or liberties, let alone someone else's. Therefore, why would you believe that they would have an interest in protecting yours?

With everything that is taking place in America today; the founding fathers would be appalled. What do you think the founding fathers would say to us all, if they could? They would be yelling at the top of their lungs, *"It's your responsibility to know your rights and to protect yours and your fellow American's liberty from an out of control government!"* They would also add, "We, as the founding fathers, have given you the tools to ensure that you will have the capacity to preserve the form of government that we had given to you." Unfortunately, though, most of the American people do not find it important enough to protect their liberties, let alone protect someone else's. Just look around and evaluate what is important to most people, you'll be surprised. Most people claim to care about our country, but do not know what our country's underlying principles are. Nonetheless, people continue to declare their love for our country, but when a conversation starts leaning toward government actions their eyes glaze over and they run for the door. If the majority of the American people will not discuss the problems or actively participate in protecting another persons' rights and liberties, then there is no hope in returning the American government back to its proper role. I, however, am concerned about what is happening to our country through an out of control government. Furthermore, if we refuse to act, our complacency will hurt our children and our future freedoms even more than one can imagine. How can a system of equal justice work properly if we are not taught the truth about how our form of government is to operate? The answer is, it can't. Logical reasoning must always prevail over emotional thinking. Therefore, when a problem arises, we must first acknowledge that we have a problem and then we must address the possible solutions accordingly. There is something terribly wrong with America today and with addressing irrefutable facts it may become apparent to you as well, that's if you were not already aware. Please have an open mind and be prepared that you will be informed of some disturbing facts.

Defining Yourself
The Road To Hell Is Paved With Good Intentions

On a personal level, this is by far the most important chapter of the entire book and saving this chapter for the end, which was my original intent, wouldn't do anyone any good. Therefore, as you can see, I corrected the problem by moving this chapter closer to the beginning. Nevertheless, the key to understanding any given situation is the ability to suppress any conflicting emotional attachments so you can exercise your ability to recognize the truth for what it truly is. The largest contributing factor as to why there are so many problems that exist today within our country is that most of the American people, both within the government and that of the private sector, have lost their way. Most people have found themselves at a critical juncture, a crossroads if you will, in their life and they are completely lost. Therefore, most of the American people have no sense of direction, when it concerns the founding principles of our country. This is a direct result of the contradictions and inconsistencies that have been created and placed upon the American people by the governments, both locally and federally. Due to the lack of direction, this has created a personal void within a good portion of the American people, which has caused conflicting points of views within our society. In order to fill this void and regain direction, I recommend that you consider the principles that created our country and to conduct a personal self-assessment. Have you ever taken the time to assess your underlying principles and beliefs? Do you understand the founding principles that formed our country? Do you truly understand what your core beliefs are and as to what you stand for? If your answer is no, I would then suggest that you take the time to do so. Only then will you have the ability to recognize the cause as to why you are the person you currently are. Most of the American population is unaware that a void has been created within their composition. Some, however, have noticed the void but rather than address the issue they continue to suppress the recognition thereof. Most, on the other hand, don't know of its existence so they don't know where to begin. It is important to understand that everyone is composed of two separate dispositions, their genuine-self and superficial-self. Everyone deals with these two separate dispositions on a daily basis. A good example of this is where a person has decided to make a decision based off emotion rather than logic. All the decisions that are made based off emotional thinking, rather than using reason and logic, will have a devastating affect on your financial matters, your relationships, and your underlying principles. An emotional reaction or mindset is the primary characteristic of your superficial-self, which includes, but is not limited to, jealousy, greediness, and pride. If you allow your underlying principles to become affected by your emotional mindset, you will find yourself backpedaling trying to save what you had created. More importantly, you will find yourself trying to salvage your fundamental rights and liberties, as we are seeing today.

Now that you are aware of the two separate dispositions that exist within every person, the responsibility of making sure that your genuine-self prevails ultimately resides within you. Most of the people within our country have allowed their superficial-self to prevail over their genuine-self, which falls back on the personal void and why it was created. Most of the American population are finding themselves disregarding respectability and the Rule of Civility when interacting with other people. I have noticed, with the passage of every year, more and more people are becoming extremely self-serving. You can see this on our roads and highways because of the insults that are continually being conveyed and the aggressive driving that borders reckless endangerment. You can see how this type of behavior has become apparent in the workplace. It is appalling to see that co-workers will voluntarily and intrusively engage themselves in gossip about another out of jealousy, spitefulness, or for the lack of self-confidence. Disturbingly enough, you can also see how a good portion of our fellow Americans will not hesitate to use the force of government against their fellow Americans. This makes me sick, especially when this type of action is not warranted. As you can see, when a person allows their superficial disposition to get out of control it will almost always affect their attitude in their profession. This type of behavior is bad enough, but when it starts to affect the individuals within the law enforcement community it ultimately becomes a dangerous combination. For most of us, we can see that this is true due to the fact that the realm of customer service has been affected to the point of being almost non-existent, both within the government and the private sector. Even though this problem exists, it is more prominent in and around the major cities, within the governments of our country, and within some of the major corporations. This type of behavior is occurring because of the conflict between the two dispositions. The superficial disposition is introducing conflicting information, basically lies, to the genuine disposition. For most of us, this type of behavior was introduced to us early on in life. Early on, most of us were taught the fundamental aspects and the founding principles that created our country, which is the United States of America. What most of us were taught was an understanding of our rights, liberties, freedoms, and the protections thereof. Today, however, we are seeing contradictions and inconsistencies that have surfaced and are conflicting with what we had been taught. This brings us back to what I call, "The Rule of Civility". The Rule of Civility contains the basic principles of liberty, freedom, and respect. In addition, the American people need to recognize that The Rule of Civility, if used consistently, will secure the founding principles that created our once fair, free, and just United States of America. Basically, it will secure the American way of life, once enjoyed years ago. Even so, it appears, with the assistance of the federally subsidized public school system, that we have veered far away from this concept. With that said, let's clarify the meaning of this rule.

The Rule of Civility is the notion of a voluntary society, the foundation for mutual respect, and teachings of moral principles. The Rule of Civility should inspire each person to accept the truth for what it is and should always be used as a basis for reasoning. It should guide your conduct toward others, which means that everyone should be treated as their own king; free to do whatever they want to so long as they do not harm another during their journey. This rule ensures that the rights, liberties, and freedoms of every person will be protected and respected. It has been found to be fair, incorruptible, and morally correct. What person would not want the freedom to build a business without asking for permission, own property without government involvement, and the security of not going to jail or prison for exercising their liberty to choose when no one has been harmed in their decision? If the American people, as a whole, would just implement this basic rule every facet of our society would change for the better, both economically and equitably. What I mean by equitably is that I am implying that justice will be dictated by good reason, the use of one's conscience, and a natural sense of what is fair and just for all, not blindly enforcing unjust laws. Whenever we depart from using civility, which includes voluntary cooperation, and we turn to a false sense of security by using force, with good intentions or otherwise, the immoral value inherently associated with the use force will always prevail over good intentions. If we continue to turn our back on our responsibility to our fellow man by refusing to accept and use The Rule of Civility we will have accomplished only one objective and that is the teachings of immoral values through our actions or inactions.

Today, most of today's society is either inept (generally incompetent) or refuses to deal with the burden of clarifying the differences between their two dispositions, let alone understanding The Rule of Civility. As a result, most of the American population continually reassigns personal responsibility upon others or chooses to ignore their responsibility all together. Anyone that has chosen this path has also decided to directly or indirectly be part of the problem, which is threatening our personal freedom and liberty, by enforcing their personal beliefs or disbeliefs upon others. Most of the individuals that have found their way into a government position are accomplishing their objective by using the force that is government. This is in direct conflict with the purpose of The Rule of Civility and the Constitutions, both locally and federally, which were created to preserve the protections, freedoms, and liberties that we, as Americans, used to enjoy. One would think that life experiences would be the best example that a person could learn from; however, this is not the case for most of the American population. Sadly enough, most are uninterested in preserving another person's rights, liberties, or freedoms let alone their own. This brings me to an example of self-centeredness. Have you ever encountered a person that had totally disregarded your space and/or interrupted you, in any fashion, because they wanted to tell you a joke or to relay some type of insignificant information? If you had, this was all due to the other person's self-centeredness and, if they had continued with their interruption, their inability to see that their actions were disrespectful. The point I am trying to make is that most of the American people do not have enough discipline to control their superficial-self. Unfortunately, this affects most of the American population, especially when they believe that another has insulted them. We have absolutely reached a sad point in time when the American population continually perceives everything as an insult and that the majority of the American people are no longer offering the benefit of the doubt. More importantly, we have reached the end of America or the spirit of America when it is to be considered a crime to insult another. For informational purposes, the First Amendment of the Constitution protects the speech that may be considered unwarranted, as an insult, or any other objectionable language. The First Amendment was not implemented to protect popular speech; it's there to protect unpopular speech. Why? Well, it's relatively simple. Popular speech needs no protection due to the fact that it has everyone's approval. Nevertheless, when is concerns unpopular speech, there are four main reasons why a person would allow their superficial-self to prevail over their genuine-self and they are; adulterated power, spitefulness, cowardliness, and that of influence. Adulterated power is an addiction and I'm not speaking about the addiction of a foreign substance introduced into the body. I am referring to the sensation when adrenaline or any other endorphin has been produced and released into the body. Power, specifically adulterated power, is one of the most addictive feelings that anyone, of an immoral nature, could ever experience. The remaining three, spitefulness, cowardliness, and influence are all, in my opinion, self-explanatory.

Now that you understand the details concerning the human composition hopefully you'll never again allow your superficial-self to surface. One should always remember that when you allow your superficial deposition to prevail you have voluntarily put yourself below The Rule of Civility and have disregarded the expectations of ethics and decency, especially if you are employed by a government entity. When a person has engulfed themselves within their superficial disposition in order to fit in with their associates and/or acquaintances nothing good can come from this type of interaction. It is; therefore, based off of untruths and dishonesty. This, again, can be dangerous to the American people that reside within the private sector, especially when this type of attitude evolves within the law enforcement community. Even so, you may be saying to yourself, just because a person wants to fit in and has good intentions does not mean that they are a bad person. I would agree; however, when force is use to implement their intentions one would have to considered that if force is needed it may not be a good idea. Remember, the road to Hell is paved with good intentions. In addition, due to the enforcer's behavior, it has created an undesirable and negative affect on the people around them by setting an unworthy standard in society. Nonetheless, they will discover, sooner or later, that they will regret their decision in using force and not standing up for what they truly believe to be morally correct. A good example of this is when a neighbor of yours observes you building a shed or having a pre-built shed delivered onto your own property. Your neighbor then immediately questions himself or herself as to you having a permit for putting the shed on "your" property or not. In return, their curiosity, their need to suppress others, and their superficial-self gets the better of them. Without discussing the matter with you, they pick up the phone and report you to the zoning authorities. In this scenario, the neighbor's actions were unwarranted. Giving this person the benefit of the doubt, their actions could have been spurred by the fact that they themselves had to get a permit in order to have a shed placed on their property. Even so, two wrongs don't make a right. Yet again, this is a prime example of a person totally disrespecting their fellow American. When this type of behavior surfaces, I become confused as to the reason for their actions. Why? Again, it's quite simple. It takes more energy to be an evil and spiteful person then that of a genuinely good person, especially when it's not warranted. Yet again, in this scenario, what does the neighbor think the repercussions will be when you find out that they had called and reported you to the zoning authorities? More than likely, you and the remaining members of the community, once made aware of their harmful act, will ostracize your neighbor from the community. The inevitable part to all of this is when the neighbor notices that everyone within the community is acting differently towards them and they themselves will become even more evil and spiteful. If this were to happen, they would not be able to control their superficial deposition and will begin to spiral downward in a social collapse. I am dumbfounded as to why it is that nosey, intrusive, and spiteful people continually misunderstand why the majority of people around them no longer want to associate themselves with such a person. In order to put all of this into perspective we must understand the true cause of it all. The cause of this problem has to do with human nature, the superficial disposition, and flat-out laziness. I have already enlightened you on the specifics of the superficial disposition and laziness is self-explanatory. However, human nature, on the other hand, is a completely different matter and it needs to be addressed. Human nature functions in the same manner as electricity; it always takes the path of least resistance, particularly for those who are inherently evil, weak minded, and unhappy. We all know that it's human nature to be curious and there's nothing wrong with exercising your curiosity. However, somewhere along the way, some of the people in today's society have taken the innocents of curiosity and turned it into an intrusive and harmful act. Instead of inquiring how or why another person was able to accomplish a certain task, they engulf themselves in their anger and jealousy. Yet again, due to the void, they have either knowingly or unknowingly allowed this to affect their actions to the point that they have overstepped the boundaries of curiosity and have taken an active role in disrespecting the privacy of another.

An important point that one should always remember is that your personal problems do not cause your superficial disposition to surface. It is your superficial-self, once it surfaces, that causes the majority of your personal problems, both at home and at your place of business. Remember, anger and jealousy all stem from the void and why it was created, which I'll explain in a moment. Nonetheless, we cannot ignore the fact that this problem is occurring on an enormous scale and, as a result, the remaining genuinely goodhearted people are left to cope with the consequences of the actions taken by these malicious individuals. When these malicious individuals find themselves in an authoritative position, such as a law enforcement officer or government official, they now have the ability to force their malicious behavior onto others, unlike that of a spiteful neighbor. In the case of the spiteful neighbor, you have the liberty not to associate or involve yourself with them in any fashion. This, however, does not apply to a government entity or its employees. Today, when a government entity forces itself upon you or a loved one, you do not have the option to disassociate yourself from that entity. That is unless you are unwilling to relocate and relinquish what you have created and/or obtained. Therefore, if you want to remain in your community and keep what you have earned and/or created there is no escaping the unjust actions of such an entity. This brings us to a very important question. Do you have the right and liberty to disassociate yourself from someone you do not like or feel safe around? Did you answer yes? If so, why is it that we do not have the right and liberty to disassociate ourselves from an unsafe, corrupt, and immoral government? The intent of our country, when the founders formed the Constitution and implemented the government thereto, was not to put the people in the private sector at the mercy of any one of the governments, federally or locally. The intent and purpose was to protect us from malevolent (evil) people, including those that have found themselves within a government entity. Even though this is true, what is a person to do when malicious people have found their way into a government position like that of a politician, a judge, or even a law enforcement officer?

This is a good time to explain the void and why it was created. Do you recall when I stated that this all started for us at an early age? I said that for a reason. The American people are coming to the realization that they have been lied to. Most of the population has always seen the contradictions and inconsistencies; however, they have never been taught the proper way in correcting the injustices. Most of the American people have come to a point in their life where they have given up on trying to understand or resolve the injustices, which have been contributed by the lies, inconsistencies, and contradictions. This is mostly due to the fact that they themselves do not know how to articulate, address, or let alone offer a solution for what is wrong. In some cases, they do; however, fear has forbidden them from going forward with their solution. As for a good portion of the American people they do not know, without any uncertainty, as to what they can do legally; they only know what the governments are forcing them to do and as to what is illegal. This is the void. The void consists of inconsistencies, contradictions, and uncertainties with the laws. This is where the problem begins. It's sad to say that most of the American population has no idea as to what they are able to do legally. Therefore, when a person does not know, without any uncertainty, as to what they can do legally; their ambitions, ideas, and even their dreams will mostly be destroyed. Moreover, the void also consists of the dictatorial hearsay that contributes to the uncertainty and is continually being conveyed upon us day in and day out. Dictatorial hearsay is when a person of authority enforces a rule or law based off of a rumor or someone else's misunderstanding and then disseminates a legal opinion concerning such rule or law, all without reading the law for themselves. They have literally placed the foundation of their entire beliefs system within hearsay, as opposed to the rule of Law itself. This is why the laws seem to change constantly. Remember, what is legal today may not be legal tomorrow. More importantly, when such a person has decided to spread such falsehoods or misrepresentations they themselves have committed a crime. Due to their official capacity, their lies and deceptions have not only caused a harm to the people around them, but has also caused a harm to the rights, liberties, and freedoms that the American people possess. This, for all intents and purposes, is considered to be treason. Moreover, it is treason against the document in which these principles have been secured, the Constitution of the United States of America. Therefore, I am once again dumbfounded as to why these individuals are not charge with treason, let alone charge with practicing law without a license.

Even though some would disagree, I am sure that they are feeling the effects of the void nonetheless. The effects of the void are; the lack of direction and not knowing where one stands with the rules of our society. This creates fear, animosity, and the feeling of being betrayed by your fellow Americans. There is, however, an additional effect that most of us refuse to address or continually overlook. That's the lack of self-preservation. Self-preservation concerns your ability to keep what you have earned and/or created. I'm confused as to why it is that law-abiding hard-working Americans allow their personal wealth to be stolen from them by a socialistic mentality. It disturbs me that most of the American people, especially the youth of America, don't even know the meaning of communism or socialism. For if they did; they would truly understand why the majority of the American people have the feeling of helplessness and do not know where to turn for help. Therefore, let me make one thing clear; forcing your will upon others and the taking another person's property by force, with the threat of imprisonment, is always wrong! With that said, have you ever claimed to be a patriot or that you were being patriotic? Did you answer yes? If so, what are you being patriotic about? Are you being patriotic about socialism or is it that you're being patriotic about freedom and liberty? You really need to think about your answer before you commit to it, because most people don't know the difference. If you have chosen freedom and liberty then be a true patriot and protect your fellow American's life, liberty, property, and freedom. If we allow the foundation of America to be destroyed, how can we then be expected to build a future? It is frustrating to see that most of the American people are trying to cope with the consequences of the lies and injustices, even though they don't fully understand why or how this is happening to them. Some do understand; however, they are afraid to speak their mind. Some, on the other hand, are in a state of disbelief, because they themselves cannot believe that their government would do such a thing. That's if they haven't already reached the point of realization.

With that said, there is one last aspect that needs to be covered. In order for you to fully understand the cause of the void or any other problem in your life you must go through the six stages of recognition. It is a fact that you're going to go through these stages no matter if you believe you are or not. It's just a matter of how far you are willing to go. I say this because; some people do not possess the discipline to complete the journey. Still, there are some that do not believe that such a journey exists. In order to prove that the journey exists all one has to do is become aware of the stages. For that reason, the stages of recognition consist of; shock, confusion, denial, anger, depression, and then realization. Again, most people do not make it past the anger stage. Sadly enough, some make it to the depression stage, that's if such an event warrants depression. If so, that's where the journey ends for some. On a positive note, a good portion of the population possesses the ability to complete the stages of recognition and I believe you can as well. Once you have completed the journey only then will you be in a position to take action and go forward with resolving the problem at hand. Therefore, the information that I have just provided you should be of some assistance with reading the remaining chapters of my book. In addition, it will help you regain the foundation for identifying the truth and will assist you with the ability to overcome and adapt to any given situation. All you have to do is be honest with yourself and your genuine-self will always prevail. In accomplishing this intent, only then will we return to the freest, wealthiest, and most prosperous country in the world. It all starts with one person at a time.

What Have We Become

"None are more hopelessly enslaved as those who falsely believe they are free." *Johann Wolfgang von Goethe*

During the early years of our country, the so-called land of the free, most of the American people had finally recognized that slavery was wrong. The people of the time had corrected this immoral injustice on humanity and passed it down from generation to generation in the form of a Law, the 13th Amendment to the Constitution of the United States. The 13th amendment only has two sections and it states as follows:

> SECTION 1. *"Neither slavery nor involuntary servitude, except as a punishment for crime whereof the party shall have been duly convicted, shall exist within the United States, or any place subject to their jurisdiction."*
>
> SECTION 2. *"Congress shall have power to enforce this article by appropriate legislation."*

I would like to draw your attention to the words "involuntary servitude". What do you think involuntary servitude means? Well, in order to completely understand the meaning, let's go to Black's Law Dictionary and define it.

> Involuntary Servitude means; *"The condition of one forced to labor – for pay or not – for another by coercion or imprisonment."*

Now that we have that behind us, what I am about to cover is very simple. There is no disputing the fact that involuntary servitude is slavery[1]. Therefore, does voluntary servitude constitute slavery? No, it does not. This is true due to the fact that the service or servitude that is being rendered is being done so voluntarily, which means that the person that is submitting to the servitude would have had to entered into such an agreement knowingly, willing, and voluntarily. A good example of this arrangement can be seen in our Military and, believe it or not, in the workplace. Despite the fact that slavery has been outlawed it somehow still exists today. For anyone to think otherwise would have to be introducing a nonsensical idea or mindset. Therefore, there are only two differences between the slaves of the early years and that of the American people today. Even though you may have a need to exchange your labor for a form of currency, on an hourly or salary basis, these differences still exist. Whoa, hold on a second. You're probably asking yourself, is he leaning toward a conclusion that slavery exists today because I have a job? You are absolutely correct, I am. Even so, you are not a slave just for the mere fact that someone else employs your labor nor are you a slave because you have decided to convert your labor into a form of currency. Nevertheless, the American people are indeed slaves. This is because of two organizations, like that of the slave owners of years past, that is forcibly extracting a large percentage of your wealth and, like most people, you believe that you cannot do anything to

---

[1] Slavery means; *"The practice of keeping individuals in such a state of bondage or servitude."*

stop it. Long ago, I reached the conclusion that slavery absolutely exists today within our country and not only as a punishment for committing a crime, but for the fact that the government can forcibly take a portion of your income all without your say. How immoral and wrong is that?

Today, there are only two major differences between the American people and that of the slaves of the early years. We have a bigger plantation to roam and the governments of our country determine how much of a slave we are. With that said, I believe I need to elaborate a little further, even though these differences may be self-explanatory. To do so, I must refer to involuntary servitude. Remember, involuntary servitude means; one forced to labor, for pay or not, for another, which can be done by coercion or imprisonment. It is important that you remember this definition. Furthermore, I must clarify that my next question does not apply to you if you are currently incarcerated. It only applies to the people that think they are free. With that said, here's the question. Has all the American people been imprisoned? Did you answer no? Then why is it that the Federal, State, and local governments believe that they deserve part of your income, outside of lawful sales/indirect taxes that they collect, and believe that they have a need to regulate you heavily? I ask this, which may seem to be an absurd question, because of a few important facts. This is what happens to inmates during their incarceration. No matter if you work for an employer or if you are self-employed, you may believe the law requires you to spend hours of your time and labor working to pay an income tax, which is slavery in itself. If an inmate works and is compensated for his or her labor the government takes a portion to pay for their incarceration. Again, when did we, as a whole, become incarcerated or, more importantly, when did we become coerced?

On a personal note, I want you to know that I am not just making an argument about the income tax, there is more to this than the tax itself. The income tax, along with inflation, are nothing more than mechanisms that have been designed to keep us enslaved to the bankers by using the force of government to accomplish their intent. In order to prove my assertions I call upon your logical sense and your genuine disposition. You probably didn't realize how important the chapter titled "Defining Yourself" would be and why I would even write such a chapter. Now you do. Nevertheless, all you have to do, once your eyes have been opened, is to take a closer look at "our" system of taxation and you will see how it has been designed to be misapplied in order to keep most of us broke so that we cannot save for our future, educate our families, and defend ourselves. Why do I say such a thing? The reason is simple. How can you control someone that has wealth and/or is self-sufficient? The answer is, you cannot. What most people do not see is that a slight of hand has taken place that has tricked the American people in to turning over a good portion of their wealth by offering them something of lesser value in return. The problem starts with the coercion and lies that have been perpetrated upon the American people. The coercion, that I believe exists, starts with obtaining a Social Security Number and the filling out and submitting a thing called a tax return. There are other causes, but I will cover them in the following chapters. If the American people would just ask themselves this next question, the truth about being a slave or not will be answered. Are you compensated for your time and labor for filling out such a document? No, you're not. In addition, if you don't know how to fill out the tax document you'll have to pay someone else to do it for you. Again, if you are required to fill out the government's tax documents, all without being compensated, and the government forcibly takes a significant portion of your income, by way of a direct tax on your labor, how is this not forced labor for another? It is forced labor, which constitutes slavery, no matter how you look at it. Another part that also applies to the tactics of coercion, which have been implemented by the government and the socialists within, is that you have been brainwashed into permitting your property to be withheld from you, on a regular basis. The important point to remember is that your money represents your labor and your wealth. Consequently, if you were to hire someone to assist you in filling out the tax documents you'll have to pay for their services, it's not free. Either way, your labor and wealth will still be extracted from you; therefore, you'll pay for it physically or monetarily in the same manner as a true slave. Remember, you're not filling out and filing these tax documents because you want to. You're doing so for the government agencies and because you believe that the law requires you to do such. However, the last statement is not true. You are doing all the above out of hearsay and fear. Fear and hearsay that has been instilled in you and, due to ignorance, has been circulated and reinforced by your fellow Americans, which by the way was all created by "your" government. This is exactly what the slave owners of years past had to achieve in order to keep their slaves in line. For crying out loud, this is exactly what Hitler had to achieve in order to create his fascist State, which included controlling the people of Germany through the use of fear and punishment. Therefore, you and almost every other American are acting in the same manner as a true slave, with the belief that you'll be punished for not complying with your master's wishes. The sad part about all of this is that there are a lot of Americans that believe the lies and are truly afraid of their own government, even though they claim to be living in a country that is nicknamed the home of the brave. How un-American is that?

What's even more disheartening is that every person, here in America, has been presented with the truth; however, they continually refuse to recognize it. I'll give you a few examples. Most people believe that they are required to obtain a social security number by submitting an application for such a number, which defies logic. Another important example is that most people believe the tax law requires their employer to withhold a portion of their wealth and property, which includes their earnings. This is in spite of the fact the withholding document needs your signature, which grants the permission to be withheld from. This again defies logic. If the tax law required you to be withheld from and requires the employer to withhold, then the law itself would grant such permission and mandate such a requirement. Your employer would never need your permission. Due to the fact your employer needs you to agree to and sign the withholding document proves that you and your employer are not required to deduct and withhold pursuant to any law. Simply put, your employer cannot lawfully deduct and withhold any of your property without you first granting such permission. That's to say that we are living within a country that is truly operating under the rule of law as opposed to the government making up the law as they go along. Even so, this is different from collecting property and sales taxes, where the State, County, or City can assess and collect all without your signature. Yet, despite all of the evidence, most people still believe that they are required to supply their signature on tax returns and many other government documents. If you are saying to yourself that he is crazy, meaning me, and that we all have to submit to this requirement, this in itself would prove that the government's lies and propaganda has removed all of your critical thinking capabilities and has truly turned you into a slave. Why do I say this? I say this for one reason only. This is exactly what the governments of our country would want you to believe and, make no mistake; they will punish you for not obeying with their wishes. This, again, is exactly how the Mafia reacted when dealing with insubordinate "customers".

It is absurd to think that a free person will be subjected to harassment, intimidation, and a punishment for the mere fact of exercising their liberty to choose and; therefore, does not comply with someone else's wishes, especially when no one has been injured. What's even more disheartening is that you know that I am stating the truth. It doesn't matter if it's right or wrong, you'll be punished nonetheless. Still, some people say that I am wrong, because most people fill out tax returns to get a refund. Some also state the authority to tax our personal labor comes from the 16th amendment. Okay, I can agree that some people fill out tax returns to receive a refund, because who wouldn't want a refund? However, the 16th amendment did not authorize a direct tax to be placed upon the American people, specifically on their labor. Why? Well, first things first. The Law, being the Constitution, cannot contradict itself. Therefore, if the 16th amendment had truly authorized the mandatory payment and collection of an Income Tax on the American people then the 16th amendment would be in direct conflict with the 4th, 5th, and 13th amendments of the Constitution, among other Articles. As a result, the United States Supreme Court[2] has ruled that our system of taxation cannot, in any fashion, be mandatory on the American people, especially when it concerns the exchange of one's personal labor for a form of currency. Furthermore, if the 16th amendment had truly authorized the implementation of a personal income tax why did the Federal government have to pass into Law the Revenue Act of 1942, also known as the Victory Tax? I ask this because the 16th amendment was passed in 1913, twenty-nine years before. There would have been no need to pass the Victory Tax, which authorized a direct tax to be placed upon the American people, during WWII.

This is extremely troubling when the IRS itself states and I quote that in, *"1931 The IRS Intelligence Unit used an undercover agent to gather evidence against gangster Al Capone. Capone was convicted of tax evasion and sentenced to 11 years."* Whoa, wait a minute. Didn't the conviction of Al Capone take place in 1931? It did. Therefore, one would have to believe that if the Department of Treasury was able to charge and convict Al Capone for tax evasion then there had

---

[2] Flora v. United States, 362 US 179, 80 S.Ct. 630 (1960), "Our system of taxation is based upon voluntary assessment and payment, not upon distraint." Stanton v. Baltic Mining, 240 U.S. 103 (1916)"…the Sixteenth Amendment conferred no new power of taxation…" Garner v. United States, 424 U.S. 648. (1975), Cheek v. United States, 498 U.S. 192. (1991), and the lists goes on and on.

to have been an income tax in effect. If this is true, why did Congress resort to passing the Victory Tax Act in 1942, which authorized a direct tax to be placed on the American people, as a whole, eleven years later? This was taken directly from the IRS' website and I quote; "*In 1939 only about five percent of American workers paid income tax*[3]. *The United States' entrance into World War II changed that figure. The demands of war production put almost every American back to work, but the expense of the war still exceeded tax-generated revenue. President Roosevelt's proposed Revenue Act of 1942 introduced the broadest and most progressive tax in American history, the Victory Tax. Now, about 75 percent of American workers would pay income taxes.*"[4] As according to the misguided believers that the 16th amendment authorized such a tax, one would have to consider that the Federal government would have had no need to pass the Victory Tax in 1942, because the government would have already had such authority pursuant to the 16th amendment, which was passed in 1913. Yet again, this defies logic. For the record, Congress passed the Victory Tax on October 21, 1942 in order to impose a direct tax on the American people within the 50 States, pursuant to the War Powers Clause of the Constitution. Al Capone was convicted for tax evasion because he had fallen within a taxable activity, unlike the majority of the American people. Needless to say, as the Constitution demands, the Victory Tax was repealed by section 6 of the Income Tax Act of 1944, two years after it had been implemented upon the American people. However, Congress failed to make the general public aware that the American people within the private sector were no longer required to assist in the war effort, by way of the Victory Tax. Therefore, the American people did not know that they could discontinue the withholding and payments to the IRS or should I say the Bureau of Internal Revenue. Once the American

---

[3] The Wealth Tax of 1935 - Those making more than $5 million a year were taxed up to 75 percent. Again, taken from IRS Website.

[4] http://www.irs.gov/app/understandingTaxes/teacher/whys_thm02_les05.jsp

---

people had continued to pay for a liability that they were no longer required to pay, the Federal government only had one alternative to consider, which was to assume and/or determine that the people must have been paying voluntarily. This is why the Federal government, along with the IRS, always addresses "our" system of taxation to be based off of "Voluntary Compliance". Contrary to popular belief, certain individuals within the Federal government and the Federal Reserve Banks knew that they could play the patriotic card on the American people and very few would ever question anything concerning the repealed Law. They knew that they could enslave the American people by using their own patriotism against them.

Interestingly enough, when a person receives a tax refund they are only receiving a portion of the money that had unlawfully been taken from them. It's as if you were being robbed and you decided to ask the person that is robbing you if you could keep some of the money. That's unless you are getting back more then what you had paid into such a scheme. If this is the case, you still have not received any government money; all you have done is taken possession of stolen property. This is true no matter if you want to believe it or not. Therefore, just because the thief had turned over the stolen property to you, this does not negate the fact that it is stolen property nonetheless. Let me make it perfectly clear, in no way is the government relinquishing any of their money or property to you. The governments of our country do not raise money in the traditional sense, they consume other people's wealth; therefore, they do not have any money of their own. The government's debt, the Grace Commission Report, and the Congress itself confirm this. Consequently, if you fill out a tax return in order to obtain a refund, common sense tells us that the request for a refund is indeed an application, which is voluntary and could very well be denied. If the taxing agency has the authority to change and/or deny a tax return that was signed and filed under the penalties of perjury and had been mandated by law, this fact also proves that the filing of such a document is voluntary. Furthermore, why is it that the governments of our country continually contradict this fact by lying to the American people by stating that such an act is mandatory? The Federal government has reported on numerous occasions and in their publications that "our" system of taxation is based off of "Voluntary Compliance". If our system of taxation is voluntary, then it cannot be mandatory. This is a classic oxymoron[5]. It appears that the Federal government has successfully used Sir Isaac Newton's law of motion, where one force meets another equal force that effectively cancels each other out, and has done so foolishly by applying it to the English language. Is this what the Federal government sought to achieve so that their statements would effectively become meaningless? The words "Voluntary Compliance", when used in a mandatory context, effectively become useless; however, if we are to take these words literally then they can only mean it is voluntary to comply. If our system of taxation was truly mandatory why didn't the government use the words "Mandatory Compliance"? Furthermore, why is it that the governments of our country have to resort to lies and the use of such misleading words? The answer is that they have to spread propaganda and untruths in order to continue their enslavement upon the American people. Still, if you decide to keep your earnings and/or wealth, as certain CEOs and government officials have done, then you cannot be punished for exercising your liberty to make that decision. Moreover, the filing of a tax return is evidence of theft, extortion, and involuntary servitude, all of which are illegal. It's sad to see that some of my fellow Americans cannot understand this concept. I am a true believer that this is all due to the fact that most people have attended public schools and have succumb (given in) to their superficial-self, which has hindered their critical thinking capabilities. More importantly, which is sad to say, most of the

---

[5] Oxymoron - expression with contradictory words. Some examples are as follows: sweet sorrow, paid volunteer, true lies. and awfully good.

American people have chosen to remain ignorant, uneducated, and have no interest in knowing or protecting the foundation of their rights, liberties, and freedoms. That, again, is un-American! Another disturbing aspect concerning the American people today is that most people do not possess the ability to distinguish between what is mandatory and what is voluntary.

A troubling fact, that should concern us all, is that most of the American people choose to ignore the voluntary nature of government applications or indeed cannot identify such a document. Most of the American people are aware of such documents, but not because they read the word "Application" on their face nor for the fact the person has taken due consideration of the document's intent, purpose, and nature. The truth of the matter is that most people become aware of a false belief and understanding when it concerns the intent and purpose of most, if not all, of the documents created by a government entity. This happens, despite the evidence to the contrary, when someone from a governmental or private organization instructs them to believe such a false statement. Therefore, I proclaim that obtaining and filling out the applications for a social security number and birth certificate are completely voluntary. Why would I make such an assertion? For one main reason, both documents use the word "Application" in their titles. The sad part is that most of the American people know that all applications are voluntary. Therefore, why is it that most of the American people believe that applications are required by law, which in itself would defy the meaning of the word application? Are you required to fill out and submit a loan application to a financial institution? No, you are not. The act of supplying personal information on a loan application only becomes mandatory when you have voluntarily chosen to seek such a loan. Therefore, it is imperative that everyone understands the difference between a voluntary request and a mandatory requirement, which must be followed in order to fulfill the request. The primary difference is that no one is required to make the request. In addition, the required procedures only become mandatory after you have submitted the application, which in itself was a voluntary act.

An important point to remember is; if you are required to sign a document, the signing requirement in itself proves the voluntary nature of the document. This also applies to becoming liable for the payment of Income and Social Security Taxes. Just compare the direct tax placed on your labor to that of property taxes. The primary difference is that you are not required to sign the government's documents in order to become liable to pay the property tax. The City, County, or State agencies will assess the tax through the assessment department, which has been duly authorized to do such. Basically, you are not forced to fill out and sign the government's paperwork, which in itself violates the 4th and 5th Amendment of the Constitution, concerning self-incrimination and to be secured in your personal effects. In addition, if you do not pay the property tax in a timely manner, the legal owner will remove you from their property. However, you will never be subjected to criminal charges nor will you be thrown into a jail or prison cell for not paying the tax nor will you be threatened with incarceration for failing to fill out and submit the government's paperwork. You are, however, threatened with this type of action when it concerns the Income Tax and the Social Security Tax. Again, how absurd is that? Nevertheless, all direct taxes, including property taxes, constitute force labor, extortion, and theft. Yet again, this contradicts the purpose of our countries' intent; where the people are to be treated as kings when it concerns the ownership of their property, including their labor. Nonetheless, it doesn't stop there. Are you familiar with the vehicle registration tax; the mandatory automobile insurance requirement; drivers licensing fees; business licensing tax, and now the national health care requirement? All of these "requirements" may lead into an arrestable offense, that's if you decide to invoke your free will and not act.

The interesting and always overlooked part, that needs to have a lot of attention drawn to it, is that all of these "requirements" require you to do something. Again, this defies logic, especially when it concerns the freedoms and liberties that we are supposed to have, here in America. It's as if you do not act, as your master wishes, you will be punished. Isn't one of the main characteristics of freedom and liberty the ability to choose to act or not? I am confused as to why we, the American people, have veered so far away from the principles of freedom and what actually constitutes a crime. You see it's quite simple. In order for a true crime to be committed, two very important elements have to be present, among others. The first is an injured party and the second is the act, which has caused harm to another person. If these essential elements are not present then no one should ever be charged or accused of committing a crime. To do so would prove insanity or flat out arrogance, which consists of a blatant disregard for the laws of our country. This, unfortunately, is occurring on a daily basis, where honest hardworking Americans are being arrested, locked up, and charged with committing victimless crimes[6]. Let me make it perfectly clear, if there is no victim there is no crime! The key to understanding when a crime has been committed is to know that there has to be an act that was preformed, which caused an injury to another person. No crime has been committed when a person decides to question the authority of a Law Enforcement Officer or has decided to videotape the Officer's actions. With that said, it is wrong for the Federal, State, and County governments to enforce their extortion practices upon the American people. Furthermore, it is wrong for the government to charge a person with a crime if the person has chosen to disassociate himself or herself from the Officer and decides to not comply with the government's demands. We either have the right and liberty to disassociate ourselves from

---

[6] Victimless Crime – "A statutory crime, such as prostitution or gambling, regarded as having no clearly identifiable victim."

unwanted and unsafe individuals or we do not. These acts, taken by government officials, are criminal in nature. More importantly, they are criminal acts in themselves. It has always confused me as to why a government official could get away with charging an innocent person of committing a crime for nothing more than standing up for their rights and liberties. How can this be happening here in America? I finally came to the realization as to why this is happening. There are a lot of immoral, unethical, and evil people in this world that seek power and enjoy using their power over others. Unfortunately, some of these evil individuals have found their way into government. With their newly acquired power of authority, they have chosen to punish us for our unwillingness to conform to their beliefs. Now I see why the Amish have kept to themselves and want no part of this socialistic system of injustices and lies. If you do not have the ability to completely own property, including your own labor, then you're a slave. If you're forced to work at another persons' will, with or without compensation, that is slavery no matter if you want to believe it or not. It really is that simple.

In order to preserve the rights, liberties, and freedoms that we possess, the American people need to come together and force the governments of this country to respect the people and to obey the Rule of Law. This includes the court rulings set forth by the U.S. Supreme Court that reinforces the fact that every person owns their own labor and property, which is not to be subjected to an unlawful, misapplied, or unproportioned direct tax. Stop living like a slave and start living like a free person. This will allow the American people to once again regain their liberty, freedom, and wealth.

Guilty Until Proven Innocent

We, as a society, are turning innocent people into criminals. Find out how.

Throughout the history of our country, there has always been an understanding, both written and unwritten, that each and every person will always retain their innocence until proven otherwise. Most of the American people are told and may still believe that we are all "Innocent until proven guilty" when one has been accused of committing a crime. This, however, is no longer true. The foundation of the American legal system is that you have the right to use the courts to clear yourself of the charges that have been brought forth against you, when being accused of committing a crime. This includes confronting your accuser and being able to bring forth any and all evidence that may prove your innocence. However, if you are forced to pay for an Attorney, court costs, and are denied the ability to confront your accuser and to bring forward the evidence that you believe will prove your innocence, how is it that we are to be considered innocent until proven guilty? Furthermore, if the government can deny us these basic principles, how can we consider them rights? What is happening today is completely unfair, un-American, and goes against the foundation of American Law. Therefore, if you were to find yourself within a courtroom facing criminal charges, would it be okay for the Judge to arbitrarily deny you the ability to present your evidence? Hopefully you answered no. Due to the fact that this is occurring, we all should be concerned about "our" legal system and what it has turned into. One of the main reasons why the governments of our country are getting away with this type of behavior is that the mass majority of the American people are completely unaware that this type of injustice is occurring. It is sad to see that our legal system, which claims to be based on equal justice, is operating contrary to its original intent. It is also sad to see that most people couldn't care less, unless they are involved in such an injustice.

Still, most people have a problem with understanding the fact that in order for you to have a right to someone else's labor or service, you must have first paid for the labor or service prior to the right existing. Only then can you seek to execute the newly acquired right. In other words, in order for you to have a right to a service, offered by a private person, private corporation, or governmental entity, you would have been required to compensate the person, corporation, or governmental organization beforehand. Therefore, in the case of using the courts, you have a right to the services offered by the governments of our country, which includes the entire judicial system. By addressing the fact that you and every other person, here in America, have already compensated the government for the use of their services can prove that we indeed have a right to use their courts. The fact that I am referring to is that you have done so in the form of paying sales and property taxes. Even though this is true, the governments would disagree. In spite of the government's disagreement, common sense tells you that I am speaking the truth. Again, even though we have the right to the courts, why would anyone want to use such a corrupt system? Therefore, why is the system corrupt? Most of the government employees have been blinded from seeing what genuinely constitutes equal justice. Congressman Ron Paul said it well when he stated, "Perhaps no important document is held in less regard in

Washington D.C., than the United States Constitution. In fact, the attitude of many Congressmen and government officials toward the Constitution consists of giving lip service to it by refusing to take it seriously. It is considered obsolete, written for agrarian economies; and our highly technological society has supposedly moved far beyond its limits. It is to be referred to only when convenient and ignored when inconvenient. Such men believe that truth is a passing fad, that principles change like fashions, and the men, particularly men who are politicians, must never be chained down by the written law of constitutions." What Congressman Ron Paul has observed is for a person, within a governmental department or agency, to believe that they can ignore the Law would prove that such a person to be dishonest, corrupt, and, more importantly, criminally minded in nature. Therefore, as you can see, this is in no way a fair system nor does it signify a system that claims to be based on equal justice. Nevertheless, if you were to take a closer look at our underlying laws, which are still on the books today, you will find them to be fair and Constitutionally correct, as they are written. The problem, which is causing our system to become unfair, is that the laws are being misapplied against innocent people. Moreover, due to the disrespect of our laws, the people within government now believe that they can past unjust and unlawful laws in spite of their oaths and the Constitutional restrictions. These two facts account for the primary reason why our system is no longer being administered correctly. Even though this is true, this in no way changes the fact the American people have compensated the County, State, and Federal governments for the use of their courts. Therefore, the additional fees and costs imposed by the government and the courts themselves are nothing more than a form of extortion and/or punishment. I say that this is a form of punishment and extortion because, due to the circumstances, this could cost you thousands of dollars, if not more. This totally contradicts the principles of being able to exercise your right to use the courts, which includes the Attorneys. If you have to pay anything at all, outside of posting bail and/or a bond, this type of requirement defeats the purpose of you paying property and sales taxes.

It is confusing, to say the least, as to why the American people are paying for the legal system twice. You see it's quite simple. Again, everyone within our country is currently paying for our legal system by way of property and excise taxes. Remember, excise taxes are all of the indirect taxes that we pay, like that of the sales tax, gasoline tax, tobacco tax, alcohol tax, tire tax, phone service tax, cable/satellite television service tax, and the list goes on and on. Don't be fooled, the governments of our country already have the funding that they need to operate. An important fact that no one should overlook is that the governments of our country will continue to get paid and/or funded no matter if anyone were to step into their offices, courtrooms, or jails. In support of this claim, I'll give you an example. If all the Law Enforcement Officers were to never issue any citations nor take anyone to jail they will all continue to get paid for their services. In addition, if no one enters a government courtroom the Judge, District Attorney, and the people involved in the court administration will also continue to receive their salaries and funds for operation. Consequently, why is it that the American people have to pay additional fees in order to retain their right to use the courts or to obtain an Attorney for their defense? It is confusing as to why anyone would have to pay for a private Attorney, especially when all of the Attorneys are officers of the court. If a government court forces you to pay for an appeal, process, or an Attorney then you do not have a right to use the courts. As for the money that you'll have to spend in order to defend yourself, that again is nothing more than a monetary punishment and, more importantly, a scheme to raise more revenues unjustly. If you have to pay out thousands of dollars before you're found guilty, how is this NOT a form of punishment or extortion? Even so, most of the American people cannot afford to pay anything at all and are forced to use an Attorney from the Public Defenders' Office. The risky part about using an Attorney from the

Public Defenders' Office is that most of these Attorneys are unwilling, uninterested, or incapable of supplying you with the best defense as possible. Most are unwilling to take into account the best interests of their "client". This, in itself, proves that if you are poor then you do have a right to the courts, which includes the Attorneys; however, you only have the right to a form of representation that is below the standard and expectations of ethics and decency. When such an Attorney is used, your defense is in jeopardy. Nevertheless, the government and most of the Judges and Attorneys have established and demonstrated that we, the people in the private sector, do not have a right to the courts nor do we have a right to due process of law. Remember, due process of law has been protected and; therefore, has been guaranteed by the Supreme Law of them all, the U.S. Constitution. Still, the Judges and the Attorneys, along with the Bar Association, have successfully fooled the American people once again. They have done so by forcing the American people into believing that they are required to obtain their own legal representation, that's if they have the funds to do so. This contradicts every aspect of our current legal system, which requires us to pay for its existence. Oh, that's right. I forgot. Most of the American people do not know nor do they care to know what the laws say or to know that they are being extorted from. Nevertheless, just because you have the money to hire an Attorney does not, in any way, mean that you are required to spend it. In addition, just because you cannot afford a good Attorney does not mean that you are not entitled to the best defense as possible. The government cannot have it both ways. So, what does this say about our so-called legal system? I believe it shows that our legal system has turned into an unjust, corrupt, and dishonest system.

Over the years, while in law enforcement, I have observed a lot of innocent people having to deal with a harsher penalty than having to pay for an Attorney, fines associated to a citation, or court costs. The penalty that I am referring to, if you or a loved one were to ever find yourself being arrested, is that you will remain in jail if you cannot make bail/bond. What's even worst and more severe is that you will now have an arrest record. Outside of the arrest record, what is so disheartening is that you will be required to remain in jail even though you have never been deemed to be a flight risk or a threat to public safety. Again, this is another example of the complete and utter disregard of our laws and that of common decency. Our system of equal justice seems to have changed to a system of extortion and incompetence. This is especially true in situations were someone is stopped by a Law Enforcement Officer; while driving on a suspended driver's license, found to be in possession of marijuana, or when someone has simply decided not to sign a traffic citation. Why do I mention these? I have done so, because all of these situations are identified as being a crime, misdemeanor, or otherwise, which are arrestable offenses. Believe it or not, you can be arrested despite the fact that you did not harm another person. Still, most of the American people are completely unaware that these illegal practices are taking place. The American people would know exactly how wrong and illegal the government's actions have become if they had only seen the confusion and heard the disbelief being portrayed by the innocent people that had their liberty taken from them and were brought into "our" jails. Even though you may not have had the chance, as of yet, to experience these injustices, there may come a time that you will.

Although I have only supplied a few examples of what may seem to be minor offenses, the common element to all of them is that no one was injured. In essence, they are all victimless crimes, which in itself has revealed a war that has been launched against the American people. Again, the primary element to any legitimate crime is that there has to be an injured party. Just because it was found that you were driving on a suspended driver's license does not in any way constitute a crime. In addition, just because the State government has decided to suspend your driver's license, for failing to pay a traffic citation or simply by mistake, does not in any way make you a worse driver than before the suspension. If, on the other hand, you disagree, then you are the perfect example of someone who believes in a false sense of security. Furthermore, one of these so-called minor offenses can ruin a person's life and cause them to spend lots of money and time in a jail cell. This is completely unacceptable! The most important question that one can ask is how can this be happening in America?

No matter how the situation may unfold, the important detail to remember is this. If you find yourself needing an Attorney because you cannot afford one, the court will appoint an Attorney from the Public Defenders' Office to represent you. This is where the problem begins. Your innocence and freedom are very important to you and to your loved ones. Therefore, you will want to have the best representation that you can obtain. According to a large percentage of people that have ever had to use a Public Defender they all know that most, not all, of the Attorneys at the Public Defender's Office are not the best Attorneys for the job. For if they were, they would NOT be working for the government. These Attorneys would have their own private practice or would be working on a career in the private sector. It's a shame, if you cannot afford an Attorney or have the ability to defend yourself, that your only option remaining is an Attorney from the Public Defender's Office. I contend that we should be able to use anyone of our choosing, Attorney or otherwise. We shouldn't be limited to the resources at the Public Defender's Office. This can be accomplished by setting fixed prices for legal representation and would close the door to the conflict of interest. You may be asking yourself, what conflict of interest am I referring to? Well, it's quite simple. If a government Attorney from the Public Defender's Office has been appointed to represent you, by whom do you think pays that Attorney's salary? You are correct again; the government that has charged you with the crime is paying the Attorney. Therefore, if the government has charged you with a crime and is now conducting the prosecution thereof, to whose best interests will the government appointed Attorney take into account? This is where the conflict of interest begins. The governments of our country should have never been given the authority to hire full-time Attorneys, as employees, for the purpose of defending the public. If you, as the defendant, have declared a need for representation, due to the fact the government was the entity that brought forth the charges, the government should always be required to pay for a non-governmental Attorney or private person to represent you. You may be asking yourself why? Just in case you have forgotten, we have already compensated the government by paying the taxes that I referred to earlier. Nonetheless, as an indigent defendant, one who cannot afford a private Attorney, the government has no problem with revealing the fact that their defense has already been paid for by the collection of taxes. However, when it concerns the majority of able Americans, the government refuses to acknowledge this fact. I wonder why? People talk about having a fair system of equal justice; therefore, how is this to be considered a fair system? If the government had not hired or employed permanent Attorneys the accused could use the allotted funds for their preferred representation. I know it may sound like a radical statement to make, but it really is that simple. Here's an easier way to look at this idea. There is an organization in America today that sells a pre-paid legal service. This pre-paid legal service is basically legal insurance. Again, I suggest that we have already paid for such a service in the form of taxes. The reason why we have the right to use the legal system, in order to resolve any conflict that may arise, is because we have already paid for it. However, the governments, both locally and federally, disagree due to the fact the government courts are charging the American people additional fees, besides that of taxes. Again, this fact should prove that such a statement is true, where the governments of our country do not believe that we have a right to the courts nor do they believe that we have the right to due process of law.

This next part is very important and for some I must cover it again, so pay close attention. If you are charged an amount of money in order to exercise a right, then it is not a right. It only becomes a right after the payment thereof and not before. If you are forced to pay for a service how can it be considered a right? A right is the idea of that which is due to a person. Therefore, the American people need to correct this injustice and stop the government from spreading propaganda that has convinced the American people that they truly have a right to the legal system, which in turn is not true due to the actions taken by the government. For those of you that might not understand, it's as if you purchased a service plan on your motorcycle and when you took your motorcycle in for service the dealership still charges you for the service. That wouldn't make any sense, would it? Just like in a service plan, if we have a right to use the courts or any other governmental service, we would not be required to pay any additional fees, etc. All of the additional fees that the local and Federal government agencies have decided to place upon the American people are bogus and are driven by greediness and corruption. The people within the governments of our country are acting like criminals, by taking your money for a service and then requiring you to pay more than what was agreed upon. That would be like the County Sheriff charging you an additional fee, outside of the property tax that you are paying, in order to take your complaint and issue a warrant for someone's arrest. That would be absurd. The government does not have the option to collect taxes from us and then charge the American people additional fees for the required services. If, for some reason, the governments cannot function on what they collect in taxes then they should downsize or close their doors, just like any other law-abiding corporation would have to do. Oh, that's right, the governments of our country are not law-abiding corporations or agencies. They are nothing more than a massive gang that is operating as the new mafia. This is a prime example as to why the law limits the government from collecting direct taxes, which does not apply to the legal excise taxes that I mentioned before.

Despite the fact that all of this is true, what is even more concerning is that the American people just stand by and allow these injustices to occur. Everyone would agree that having to pay for an Attorney is a problem in and of itself, but it becomes a bigger problem when you are found innocent of the charges that were brought against you. Why would I make such a claim? Well, for one main reason. One would have to remember that Attorney fees can be very expensive and could go into the thousands, tens of thousands, if not more. Despite the fact that you were found innocent you still have to pay for your defense, which could possibly take years to pay off. If this were to be the case, how is this not an unfair and unjust punishment for being found innocent? Again, this is absurd! To make matters worse, if during your trial you and your Attorney had notice an error being committed by the court, this would allow you to appeal your case to a higher court. If you have decided to appeal your case to a higher court, in order to resolve the error of the lower court, another problem may arise when you have file such an appeal. The appellate court, which is the higher court, may refuse to hear your case. Most, if not all, of the appellate courts believe that they have the authority to deny your appeal, on whatever basis they deem suitable. The United States Supreme Court is guilty of this action as well, as many other appellate courts. What that means, when this situation occurs, is that the appellate court has arbitrarily denied you the right of due process of law, by informing you that the court will not listen to your argument in open court. Basically, they have denied your appeal, even though you had paid for the service, paid their fees, and followed their procedures. Are we to believe that when we pay for a service, the appeals hearing and the court itself, that we are not entitled to such a service? And, if not, shouldn't we get a refund or be able to find another suitable provider? Oh, I forgot. We do not have this ability, because the governments of our country have a

Monopoly on the legal system and will use force in order to mandate that you remain a customer. It would be illegal for another person or private company to operate in the same fashion as the government. Therefore, not only does the government have a monopoly on the legal system they also have a monopoly on the use of force. Are we to accept that this is how our system of equal justice is to operate? Does this seem fair to you? This type of mentality reflects privileges and not rights! It reflects masters and their slaves; it does not reflect freedom and justice in anyway. I don't know about you, but I've always been told that we have a right to use our courts to adjudicate our conflicts; I was never taught that such a thing was a privilege.

Now that we have covered one of the aspects on how the courts are arbitrarily disregarding our due process rights, take a moment and consider this. In a criminal case, where a person has been acquitted, found not guilty, or the charges had been dropped, all of which are synonymous, then the governmental entity, including its witnesses, should have to pay all of the costs that you had become liable for. Why do I suggest such a thing? Again, it's simple. For if it had not been for the government and its witnesses, pressing wrongful charges against you in the first place, you would have not incurred any costs nor would you have acquire any debt in order to defend yourself. If we were truly living in a country that upheld equal justice then the American people would receive restitution once they were found to be innocent of the accusations made against them. Currently, in all civil cases, when a person or persons have filed a lawsuit against another they will become liable for all Attorney's fees and acceptable expenses, that's if the court makes a ruling in the opposing parties' favor. Then again, this will not happen unless the defendant requests such reimbursement or restitution. This same standard should also apply to criminal cases, where the government is unsuccessful in your prosecution. If this type of practice were to be implemented, this would allow the American Jurisprudence to once again overcome a system of nonsensical ideas, corruption, and laziness. Therefore, if the government decides to prosecute a criminal case, without doing a complete investigation or without having enough evidence to secure a conviction, then the government should be responsible for compensating the person or persons involved. Some would have the nerve to ask why. Well, for starters, the innocent person's name would have been slandered; they would have accumulated expenses, and during this unjust process would have lost an amount of wages or salary. This is not only the right thing to do; it is the honorable thing to do. When a government entity, government official, or individual person has brought forth wrongful charges they themselves should have to pay for their mistake. That's equal justice! That's why if the government decides to go forward without enough evidence and without a complete investigation that's on them and they should be liable for their actions. There should always be consequences for a governmental entity, agency, and/or the employees thereof when they decide to prosecute someone without success. This will by far reduce the amount of wrongful prosecutions and should help with keeping the governments of our country in check, so that they do not abuse their authority. Needless to say, this is not the case today.

The overall problem begins when a government official files criminal charges against another private person, all on the account of the testimony of a government witness or otherwise. The frightening truth is that most of the time charges are brought forth without a witness and without any documented evidence. Even so, once the charges have been filed, depending on the geographical jurisdiction, the Federal, State, or local governments will gain exclusive jurisdiction to proceed with the prosecution of the case. In other words, the government now has total control over what happens during that person's prosecution. Therefore, once the charges have been filed, the original person that had filed the charges will no longer have the ability to stop the government from prosecuting the person in question. Why? The governments of our country have been given the exclusive authority and power to prosecute all criminal cases. No private person or citizen has this ability. This is why the governments of our country are breaking the law by categorizing almost everything as being a crime. This; however, is completely different in all non-governmental civil cases where a private person or persons have filed a civil lawsuit, in which they retain the exclusive jurisdiction and/or right to prosecute their lawsuit. Then again, there are two exceptions to this rule. The first is when a corporation files a civil lawsuit against another corporation or private person. The corporation, just like a governmental entity, has to be represented by a licensed Attorney. Why? That's simple. A corporation is a fictitious entity; it is not a living human being who has inalienable rights protected by the Law. This is outside of the fact that the Bar Association mandates such representation. Nevertheless, the second is when a person has gone above the maximum monetary amount that he or she is seeking to receive and/or recover. In any case, if you were to take a closer look at the operations of our legal system, you will come to the conclusion that the witnesses for the government, along with the government itself, are in fact immune from punishment. This in itself is the catalyst for their abuse of power. How can anyone or any entity be immune from a civil lawsuit or face criminal penalties when they themselves have caused harm to another? Doesn't this type of action constitute a criminal act or, at the least, creates a situation that warrants a civil action against those that had committed the harm? Yes, it does! What's even worse is that a good portion of the American people continue to claim ignorance when it concerns this issue; however, under their same breath they have the audacity to suggest that the government, along with it's witnesses, should remain immune from punishment, even though a wrongful act had occurred. To believe such a thing is nothing more than lunacy. Even so, when asked as to why they would believe such a thing, they respond by stating that all governments, both locally and federally, should be immune because they are government. When I heard such a statement my heart cringed and I became sadden. To think that a good portion of the American people believe such a thing makes me question myself as to where I am living. Nonetheless, this is yet another conflict of interest and it is completely unacceptable, especially when the government has, in most cases, ruined a person's life.

Some of the American people actually believe that the governments of our country can claim immunity from prosecution when they themselves have committed a criminal act. This, again, is completely absurd and; therefore, I will prove how absurd this type of mindset is. Let's use the IRS again. The IRS and its agents are basically immune from punishment when they arbitrarily seize someone's property without first taking them to court. Now, here's the important part. Even though the IRS would disagree, court records show that when the IRS seizes a person's property their authority to do so is derived from a civil action and not from a criminal lawsuit. As a result, when the IRS has forcibly seized another person's property they have committed a crime and, in most cases, with the help from the local authorities. Therefore, this proves that government officials are wrongfully immune from punishment. The sad and brutal truth about all of this is that if the American people, within the private sector, were to stand by and do nothing in order to correct an unlawful act taken by a government entity, than the government itself is effectively immune from prosecution and/or punishment. It really is that simple.

Have we reached a point in time were it has now become acceptable for a government official to arrest and prosecute someone on the grounds of a false allegation and without a full and thorough investigation? No, you say? Then do something about it, because it is happening. Here's a thought. Would it be logical to have a law that would require the government, along with the person or persons, that had made such a false allegation to be punished for their actions by either serving a jail or prison sentence and by compensating the accused, which has now become the injured person? Absolutely it does! The government, along with the complainant, should be punished for putting you through a horrible unjust experience. Furthermore, as it stands today, the person that had filed the false allegation and/or had made the complaint is in no way forced to pay for the cost of your prosecution; outside of paying indirect taxes, that is. Today, the person that had made such a wrongful complaint is in no way liable for what is about to happen to you. Again, some people would disagree; however, they are forgetting about anonymous tips to law enforcement. What actually happens is the expense of your prosecution is turned over to the taxpayers as a whole. Again, the State and/or Federal government pays for the entire prosecution, not the person that actually made such a claim or filed such a complaint. Remember, the Federal and local governments have, what may seemed to be, an endless amount of money to prosecute you. This, however, is not the case for the majority of the American people. For the most part, your funds are more than likely limited. This, again, is another conflict of interest. Why? It is a conflict because the American people are paying for their own prosecutions. Therefore, an amount of one's wealth should never be a deciding factor as to the outcome of a trial or granting a person the ability of being able to defend oneself. There are only two deciding factors that should ever be allowed to dictate the outcome of a trial. These consist of; one having the ability to defend oneself, and an honest effort, set by the court, to bring forth the truth. Again, if we were able to return to an honest legal system, this in itself would effectively reduce the amount of wrongful lawsuits and/or charges being brought forth against innocent people. This would allow the courts the time to address legitimate cases where actual damages had occurred and would increase the speediness of our courts. It has always confused me as to why there are cases that will last for months and even years. As a former Correctional Officer, I have first hand knowledge of people entering a jail or prison facility waiting for their day in court, which takes entirely too long. In some cases, it has taken up to 10 to 12 months before certain individuals were able to get in front of a judge or into a courtroom in order to resolve their case. This is completely unacceptable, especially when we are talking about someone's freedom and their ability to be with their loved ones. Even so, I thought we have a right to a speedy trial. Oh that's right, the Constitution, the Supreme Law of them all, doesn't matter anymore. Does it? Nonetheless, the next question that should arise is why aren't the American people addressing this issue? The answer is that most of the American people do not care to correct these injustices because they themselves have not been affected by the government's actions, at least as of yet. Therefore, why would they care? Oh, that's right. THEY'RE AMERICANS, THAT'S WHY THEY SHOULD CARE! Therefore, why hasn't our legal system already been setup to compensate the accused by the accuser when the accused is found not guilty in all criminal cases? Again, it appears that most of the American people do not care about this issue until it happens to them or to a family member. However, by the time they start to care it is way too late for them. All the same, let's move on.

While some people may still believe that we, as Americans, have a right to a speedy trial, as guaranteed by the Constitution and the laws set forth by the States, I contend that we no longer have this right. I say this for one reason. If you find yourself being arrested, you should be brought in front of a judge or magistrate as soon as possible. According to most State statutes that requirement is set at 10 days. If you are arrested and kept in a jail cell for months at a time, then how can one say that you have a right to a speedy trial, let alone make the claim that you are innocent until proven guilty? If you are truly innocent until proven guilty then you should be released on your own recognizance[7], at least after the government

---

[7] Release on own recognizance: A pretrial release of an arrested person without bail, on that person's promise to appear for trial when it is appropriate to do so.

has processed you into their system. Believe it or not, the governments of our country have decided to ignore the laws, make them up as they go along, and have decided to violate the liberties and freedom of the American people, all without any consequences to their actions. Make no mistake; this is how the County, State, and Federal governmental agencies are operating today. It is sad, especially when you are sitting in a jail cell, that you do not have the ability to confront your accuser, defend yourself, or have the ability to protect your family or property. This is completely un-American! If, for some reason, you disagree with my assertion that we are no longer innocent until proven guilty, when it concerns the involvement of a governmental department or agency, then that only means that you have obviously never dealt with a governmental agency in any fashion nor have you attended a Police or Law Enforcement Academy. With that said, let's again address the Federal government and its Department of Treasury, the Internal Revenue Service, to be exact. If you believe that we are truly innocent until proven guilty, why is it that third parties like banks, employers, and, more importantly, Sheriff's Departments continually seize and/or relinquish property belonging to a so-called innocent person before they have had their day in court? This is extremely important, because not only have you not had your day in court, this administrative agency has no legal authority to seize, levy, or enforce anything upon the people in the private sector. I make such a claim because the law, their pocket commissions, and the Constitution itself all forbid such behavior from this agency. Yet, the IRS, with the assistance of the local authorities, continues to abuse the American people. Therefore, if we were truly innocent until proven guilty the banks, employers, and law enforcement agencies would never seize and/or relinquish any property, especially without a court order. To our disbelief, these unlawful acts are occurring. This, again, is extremely sad due to the fact these agencies' actions are undoubtedly criminal in nature. What's even more terrifying, which reminds me of a German Gestapo tactic, is that the people within the Internal Revenue Service never obtain a legal court order nor do they care to. The IRS knows that the majority of the American people are afraid of them. Therefore, this allows an IRS agent the ability to use intimidation and the threat of force to get what they want and/or what they believe they need. The only reason why the American people are not addressing this type of criminal behavior is because the American people are afraid of their own government. Ironically enough, the same government that was implemented to protect the people is now committing criminal acts against them. In fact, a lot of what they are doing is forbidden. It is not only forbidden by the law itself, but by common decency and civility. Therefore, with that said, the Federal government, along with certain local authorities, have successfully engage themselves in a war against the American people and their goal is to take whatever they want, no matter the consequences. These agencies will continue to misapply the law, in order to maintain their power and extortion practices, even though they are placing innocent people at risk of losing everything. This is nothing more than a Mafia mentality and it needs to end. However, their behavior will never end until the American people wake up and stand against this type of tyranny.

Due to the criminal organizations of years past, which were associated to the crime families and their syndicates, it appears that the governments of our country have become the beast that they were once fighting against. It has never been okay for a crime family to have dealings in loan sharking, the murdering of innocent people, and stealing anything they could get their hands on, from whomever they could. Therefore, why is it okay for the government to do the same thing? Today, the governments of our country are acting in the same manner as the fascists and communistic governments of years past, like that of Germany under the rule of Adolph Hitler. When will the insanity stop?

One of the primary reasons why government agents, like that of the Internal Revenue Service, appear to have immunity from being punished for their criminal behavior is due to a legal term which is refer to as "plausible deniability". Plausible deniability is a situation that a person can use to deny knowledge of any particular truth that may exist, because he or she is deliberately made unaware of the truth so as to shield the person from any personal responsibility associated through the knowledge of said truth. Plausible deniability is a legal concept that many Attorneys use today and, due to their political involvement, have brought forth a lower standard of ethics and integrity with the use thereof. This is why they, meaning government officials, agents, and Attorneys, rarely put anything controversial in writing. This is also why most government officials often refer you to talk with an underling of theirs or to a bureaucrat so that they can plausibly deny knowledge of the conversation or be able to say that the underling or bureaucrat misstated their position. Therefore, in order to accomplish their intent of robbing the American people, while maintaining plausible deniability, the IRS and its agents always send out unsigned, uncertified, misleading, and illegal documents to third parties requesting the seizure of one's property. When their requests are not met, their thugs will arrive on the doorsteps of not only the third party, but onto the victim's as well. This, again, goes against the intent of our country and, more importantly, the laws themselves. Could it be that the Federal government and its agencies are breaking the law everyday in order to institute a system of socialism? It wouldn't be hard to believe if in fact you have taken into consideration all of the other illegal acts that have been perpetrated by the governments, both locally and Federally? Still, how can the Internal Revenue Service or any other taxing agency file a judgment lien against an American person without first being required to take their case into a court of law? Some would say they do and that the taxing agencies obtain such authority from the Tax Courts. However, this is simply not true. For informational purposes, the taxing agencies obtain their authority to file such a lien from a statute, which is in direct violation of the 14th amendment of the U.S. Constitution. Wherein no person shall be deprived of life, liberty, or property without first being given due process of law. Therefore, the taxing agencies are misapplying their statutory authority to file these liens because the statute only applies to corporations and anyone that would fall under a taxable activity, which does not apply to the American people. Even if the Tax Courts were to issue the authority to file such a lien, they would have done so in error because the Tax Courts are NOT courts of law. They are nothing more than an administrative agency. As a result, the taxing agencies never gain the proper authority to file such a claim. As you are now aware, a lien filed by the Internal Revenue Service is not a judgment lien, it is a statutory lien that violates the U.S. Constitution and is not certified or attested to under oath, which is required by law. Only a court of law, which has proper jurisdiction, has the authority to impose such a lien. With that said; take this into consideration. How is it that you would be able to defend yourself against the Internal Revenue Service when all of your money has been taken from you? This would include inhibiting your ability to borrow due to the unlawful lien that had been filed against you. Needless to say, you'll have trouble getting the funds for your defense. Still, if the IRS or any other taxing agency can legally take your money by way of a third party, like an employer or a banking institution, then you do not have the right to own property, confront your accuser, or the right to due process of law. Again, it really is that simple.

At this point, I would like for you to take into consideration this next statement. If the IRS truly believes that you owe an amount of money and they truly want you to settle your debt, then the IRS or any other taxing agency would never resort to damaging your ability to pay. Therefore, why are the taxing agencies set out to ruin people's lives? Their criminal behavior doesn't make any sense, that's if we are to believe that the governments of our country would truly like for you to be a repeat customer. Due to the illegal actions taken by these agencies proves that they do not care about the truth nor do they care about your well-being. For if they truly cared for their fellow Americans they would not have resorted to their criminal and damaging activities. This in itself proves that this agency, among others, knows that what they are doing is wrong, which reinforces their need for plausible deniability. They all know that there is no legal requirement for any private person to pay their extortion fees. Again, if there were a law and/or legal requirement for the private person to pay the tax, then the Internal Revenue Service's attitude and behavior toward the American people would be met with reason and leniency, just as they do with major corporations. This is why the agents of the Internal Revenue Service have to resort to obtaining your property illegally? For if these agencies were to allow you to fully exercise your due process rights, the truth would be revealed and their gig would be up.

The primary reason why the governments of our country have chosen to arbitrarily ignore the laws, rights, and liberties of the American people is due to the fact that the American people have become too divided, weak minded, and afraid of their own government's intimidation tactics. In the absence of strong liberty minded individuals, how can we have a moral society, which is supposed to limit the unauthorized actions of our governments? It's simple, we can't! We are either living in a society that has chosen to have rules, which includes abiding by the U.S. Constitution, or we have reached a point where it is okay for the government to commit criminal acts upon the American people, all in the name of safety and enforcing unjust laws. Furthermore, the same excuses that are being used today to justify the unlawful actions taken by the governments of our country are the same excuses that the soldiers used within Germany's Gestapo when they had robbed, jailed, and killed innocent people. These excuses consist of, "It's the Law" or "I'm just doing my job". These same excuses, which are still being used today, are unacceptable, to say the least. What has become apparent is that we are now living within a society that requires the people, in the private sector, to follow the laws while the people within a governmental department or agency can ignore them all together. Furthermore, it appears that they can now interpret the laws in such a way the best benefits them and their department, all without having to take their case into a court of law. Consequently, if the government can do whatever it wants to the American people, who is the master and who are the public servants?

The Jury

When the founding fathers had created the Constitution, which had formed the Federal government, they put in to place certain checks and balances that would restrain the government from getting out of control. Since the creation of our country, the people have always had the ability and duty to watch over the government. The founding fathers knew that the government would never keep itself in check and would try to overstep its authority by intervening in the lives of the American people. In order to keep this country free, the responsibility of keeping the governments of our country within their assigned responsibilities and from breaking the laws themselves was left in the hands of the people in the private sector. It had been deemed so important that this power was retained and protected by "We The People", in the creation of our laws. Therefore, out of all the checks and balances that have been created and guaranteed to the American people, there are at least two that every person should be aware of. These consist of the Direct Taxation Clauses within the Constitution and the ability of the people, as jurors, to nullify any given law. The ability to nullify a law, as a jury, is called Jury Nullification. In order to impress upon you the importance of these two checks and balances, I'll explain both. The first is the Direct Taxation Clauses contained within the Constitution. These clauses were created for a reason and should have never been ignored by the American people. The purpose of these clauses was to limit the government's ability to extract property and wealth from the American people. In turn, if the people within the Federal government were to believe that they have a need to extract money from the American people, by way of a direct tax being implemented upon them, the government is required by Law to send a proposal for the proposed tax to the States. If approved by the States, the Federal government is only authorized to tax the States directly, not the people. In addition, all direct taxes imposed by the Federal government must be apportioned among the 50 States, as according to their population. The reason for this Constitutional requirement is so that a State with a lower population will not be mandated to pay more of the tax burden than that of a State with a higher population. More importantly, the taxing clauses were implemented as a legal requirement, once they were written into the Constitution, to limit the taxing power of the Federal government and, more importantly, was implemented to ensure that the Federal government would not have the ability to tax the people directly. The founding fathers knew that if the Federal government had the ability to control people's lives, with the imposition of a direct tax like that of the Income Tax, the Federal government would irreparably destroy the lives of the American people. The founding fathers knew that the power to tax is undoubtedly the power to destroy!

The Federal government has the authority to tax certain items like gasoline, firearms, and the income (profits) of corporations, which are all indirect sales taxes, but they do not have the Constitutional authority to mandate a direct tax placed upon the American people or their labor. Even so, you may be saying to yourself, isn't the Federal government currently taxing the American people directly? Yes, for the most part, they are. The Federal government was able to side step the Constitutional requirements and its limitations by creating a tax that in its nature is voluntary, which can be proven by the signing requirement. Therefore, when the Federal government and its agencies have decided to press charges against a person, living and working within the borders of our country, for not paying and/or not filing their paper work they are literally breaking the Law. This is all due to a few dishonest people within the Federal government that actually believe that the passage of the 16th Amendment of the Constitution gave the Federal and State governments the authority to tax the American people's property directly, which includes their labor. This, however, is not the case and the Supreme Court has ruled accordingly. Even though the Law forbids the Federal government from taxing the people directly, they are doing it anyway. Again, why? Well, I suggest that we, the people, are not keeping the Federal government in check with the provisions of the Constitution. Despite that, if the people within the States disagree with the Federal government's proposal to implement a new tax, they will disallow the funds. Interestingly enough, due to the request from the Federal government for the proposed tax, the American people would now be directly aware of what the Federal government had planned to spend the money on. More specifically, the American people would be directly aware of what the Federal government was trying to create or accomplish. Needless to say, these Direct Taxation Clauses have been circumvented. Yes, circumvented! You'll see how the Federal government has circumvented the Supreme Law of our land in an upcoming chapter titled, "The Truth About Inflation and Banking".

The second security measure or "check and balance" that was guaranteed to the American people is Jury Nullification. This one is by far the most important of all of the checks and balances that we, as Americans, possess. Why is that? For one main reason, it's our last chance to keep our country free, by keeping the governments of our country within the rules of their operating agreements and the laws of our society. The rules of the government's operational agreements are spelled out in plain English within the Federal and State Constitutions and within the laws made pursuant thereto. Without these rules, we would be defenseless against an out-of-control and corrupt government. It is simple to see that if a law had been passed which is in direct conflict to any one of the Constitutions, then that law is not a law. This is why the jury process is so important; however, it will never work unless the American people are educated on these facts. Even though you, as a juror, have the obligation to judge the facts of any given case, it is important that you are aware of your ability to judge the law itself. It is imperative that we, as jurors, understand that we have the duty and the responsibility to understand what our rights and abilities consist of. The primary reason is because there are far too many laws that will turn an innocent person into a criminal, all without an injury occurring to another person. Whenever the time arises, remember this. You, as a juror, will hold other people's freedoms and liberties within the palm of your hand and; therefore, due diligence will be a must.

Over the years, I have wondered why the public schools had not taught us about these issues? More importantly, why is it that hardly anyone is being taught to understand their rights, the U.S. Constitution, and Jury Nullification, among others? Could it be that the governments of our country do not want the American people to know what their protections and abilities consist of? Some people state that government officials despise it when someone from the private sector challenges their authority. Due to my experience within government, I would have to agree that most, not all, of government officials become very upset when their authority is challenged. A good example of when the people had challenged the government's authority was during the years of the 1930s, when Alcohol Prohibition still existed. Years before 1933, the Federal government had passed a law making the manufacturing, sale, and consumption of alcohol illegal and the American public finally had enough of this unjust law. From that point forward, the American people took it upon themselves to get rid of the prohibition of alcohol. The American people had accomplished this by serving as jurors on criminal cases that were brought against someone whom was being charged with a violation of the alcohol prohibition law. The American people had found the person or persons not guilty, even though there was an existing law that prohibited ones involvement in the use of alcohol. As you can see, it is easy for the American people to abolish any law that we find to be unjust, that's if we are educated on the principles of Jury Nullification. Therefore, let's take a moment and legally define what Jury Nullification is. Jury nullification is defined as, "A jury's knowing and deliberate rejection of the evidence or refusal to apply the law either because the jury wants to send a message about some social issue that is larger than the case itself or because the result dictated by law is contrary to the jury's sense of justice, or fairness." *Taken from Blacks Law Dictionary, 7th Edition.* Despite the fact that we, as jurors, have the right and duty to judge both the facts of a case and the law itself, an organization that is part of the government known as "Homeland Security" disagrees. If you believe that you, as a juror, have the right to judge both the facts and the law itself, according to some State's "Homeland Security" agencies, you are now to be considered a domestic terrorist. Although I am only listing one specific State's website, there are other States and Federal government agencies, like the FBI, that have adopted this philosophy. However, to keep this short, I am only listing one. The following has been taken right off of the State of Pennsylvania's website titled: TERRORISM, Awareness and Prevention, **(www.pa-aware.org)**

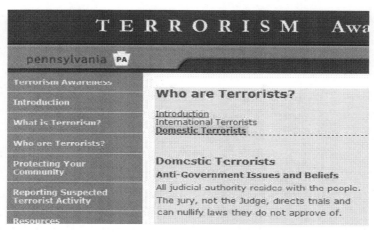

As you can see, the State of Pennsylvania has stated that if you believe that "The jury... ...can nullify laws they do not approve of" then you are to be considered as a domestic terrorist. Common sense tells us that any group of people, who are serving as jurors, can nullify a law by finding the accused person or persons not guilty. That's simple to understand. However, most of the governments and their agencies, like that of the State of Pennsylvania, has tried to convolute and complicate this issue by adding false concerns like that of "All judicial authority resides with the people" and "The jury, not the Judge, directs trials". No one believes that the jury directs a trial, that's the job of the Judge. Due to the misguided issues, we can see that this is an attempt to confuse the reader and to construe "Domestic Terrorists" out of true Americans that actually know the law and who believe in jury nullification. Can you believe that one of the 50 American States, namely Pennsylvania, would make such an assertion? Out of all the checks and balances that have been put into place, in order to keep the governments of our country in line, this is the most important tool at our disposal. If anything, it's the last counter measure that we have to correct an injustice that had been committed by any one of the governments of our country. It's a wonder, after reading Pennsylvania's website, that jury nullification still exists today. The governments are once again telling the American people that if you believe in the idea of freedom and justice that you are now to be deemed a domestic terrorist. This is only one of the total six beliefs listed on the State of Pennsylvania's website. If I were to ever meet anyone from the State of Pennsylvania's government, that had created this page on their website, I would have to ask them a two part question. That is; do they believe in the United States of America and, more importantly, do they believe in the concept of having rules and laws that govern the government? If they were to answer no, then they should be immediately removed from their position and prosecuted for treason. Either way, I will never live in nor will I conduct business in the State of Pennsylvania. No one can deny the fact that we as jurors have the right to judge the law. As you can see, some States like Pennsylvania believe differently. These States apparently do not believe in our system of justice nor do they believe in the principles that formed the United States of America. It is also apparent that none of these States believe in the Constitution, due to the fact that these organizations have put these types of statements on their websites and in their pamphlets. I suggest that the Constitution, in their eyes, is no longer applicable and that these entities have now engaged themselves in communistic activities. They themselves have become the terrorist! How can we as good Americans allow the governments of our country to make such statements, make such claims, and take such actions all without being punished for treason? What has happened to our ability, as free people, to distinguish between what is right and wrong? Traitors of our country have entered the ranks of our government and with their newly acquired power have successfully suppressed the American people's ability to see and understand the truth. Therefore, we better wake up soon...

"Paying Your Debt To Society"

and/or "Doing Your Time"

"Paying your debt to society" or "Doing your time" are two of the most popular terms used when it concerns someone being convicted of a crime and sentenced to spend an amount of time in a jail or prison cell. It's more than likely you have heard of at least one, if not both, of these phrases. Therefore, if you were to ever find yourself being accused of committing a crime you should have the opportunity to take your defense to trial. Needless to say, being able to take your defense to trial is a fundamental right that every person has, at least within the United States of America. This right is indispensable, especially for a free society. The ability to take your defense to trial is part of due process, which has been guaranteed to the American people. If you were to ever find yourself having to be in a courtroom defending yourself, what do you think will happen if the court renders a guilty verdict against you? The court will sentence you to serve time in a County, State, or Federal facility. This means that your freedom and liberty will be taken away from you, by force if necessary. Still, once you have served "your" time the government will then release you back into society. At that point, unless you were released on a government program like parole, community corrections, or State Probation that should be the end of the infringements that were placed upon your rights and liberties as a free person. However, the governments continue to implement and/or promote a false sense of security that most of the American people are unaware of. What I am referring to is when a governmental department or agency has release a person who had previously been incarcerated and states that he or she no longer has certain rights, as previously held before their incarceration. These affected rights include, but are not limited to, the right to vote and the ability to own a firearm. The reason why the governments allege that they have the authority to remove these particular rights is due to the fact that the government believes that people who have been previously incarcerated still present a threat to either themselves or to the safety of the public. This is absurd, especially when they have decided to release the person in question. If this were true, both reasons would warrant the government to reconsider releasing such a person back into society. I suggest that there is another reason for their unwarranted restrictions. The governments of our country are being instructed to implement such restrictions in order to limit the American people's rights, liberties, and freedom. By whom, you may be asking? Well, you will soon find out.

The truth of the matter is this, if the government did not believe such absurdity, that such a person still poses a threat, then why would they implement such restrictions? Furthermore, if the government truly sees their restrictions as a form of punishment, then their actions are completely illegal. Why? It, again, is simple. It is illegal for the governments of our country to place any person within the scope of double jeopardy[8]. Either way, when the governments of our country try to enforce some ridiculous provision like this, any person with common sense can see that the governments should have reconsidered the option of not releasing such a person as opposed to trying to enforce a limitation upon their free will. It is disappointing that the governments of our country would release dangerous people back into society. If a person truly poses a threat then the governments should keep them in jail or prison, but that is to say that they present such a threat to begin with. Nevertheless, it's simple to understand. If the government had decided to free such a person then that person is exactly that, FREE. The sad part about all of this is that most of the American people, including those in government, have been brainwashed into believing that the government can somehow take away certain rights from individuals that had once been incarcerated. This is completely absurd. Isn't the intent and purpose of the jails and prisons to do exactly that? Even though the government may have good intentions, it is foolish to believe that such a restriction will work on a harden criminal or someone who is truly criminally minded. To believe otherwise would prove you to be naive, ignorant, and possibly insane. Just because a government entity has told a person that he or she cannot own a firearm does not mean that person will not obtain one. This is a good example of the false sense of security that I had referred to earlier. All the same, there is one exception that would grant the government the authority to make such a claim and invoke such a restriction. This, again, is when a person has been released on a government program, which indicates that such a person has not completed their sentence of punishment.

---

[8] The Double Jeopardy Clause of the Fifth Amendment guarantees that no person shall "be subject for the same offense to be twice put in jeopardy of life or limb." The Clause provides three separate protections for criminal defendants, which include protection against reprosecution for the same offense after an acquittal, protection against prosecution for the same offense after a conviction, and protection against multiple punishments for the same offense.

This is also a good example of where logical reasoning prevails over emotional thinking. No government agency or entity has the legal authority to tell you that you cannot defend your family, vote for the person that you want in office, or obtain a good paying job, especially when they have declared you to be a free person by releasing you. Again, to think otherwise would prove lunacy. The problem starts with the elected officials and their laziness, lack of studies, and their complete disregard for other people's rights and liberties. Now, take notice, just because I only specified elected officials, this does not in any way exclude or excuse the American people from their laziness, lack of studies, or their complete disregard for other people's rights and liberties. They are just as guilty as the elected officials. Apparently, most of the American people, including government employees, do not understand that when a person has been released back into society the act of releasing such a person automatically re-establishes their status as a free person. As a result, there should be no more restrictions placed upon anyone's free will to exercise any of their protected rights or liberties that is once they have paid their debt to society. Again, for clarification purposes, this only applies to a person that has in effect completed the full term of "their" sentence. The confusion starts with you being told a half-truth, by a government agency. The premise is that, if a person has been convicted of a felony, they no longer have, even after their release, certain rights. The truth of the matter is that this only applies to a person that is either currently incarcerated or, more importantly, has been released under the supervision of a government program. It doesn't matter what type of felony it is, because when you are either incarcerated or under the supervision of a government program you have not successfully, as of yet, regained your status as a free person. It should be undeniable, after you have completed your sentence or government program, that you automatically regain your freedom, rights, and liberties. At no time should a government agency have the power to abolish any of your rights or liberties outside of sentencing you to do time within a jail or prison cell. This is punishment enough; however, if it is not then DON'T RELEASE THEM! The lies begin when we are all told that once you "do your time" or "pay your debt to society" you're now a free person. Today, however, that couldn't be further from the truth. What makes matters even worse, in some States, once you have been convicted of a felony you no longer have the right to hold a professional license like that of a nurse, electrician, or plumber. Not only will your "right" to obtain a professional license be removed, you will have a hard time getting any type of employment due to your felony conviction. I am not saying that it will be impossible for you to find employment, but it will be extremely difficult. Therefore, the next question that should be asked, is why? The problem is the government, which has made your criminal record available for public viewing. This brings me to a very well hidden process not known to many in the private sector. What I am referring to is the ability to have a felony charge expunged from your record. When you, as the felon, have filled out the proper application, pay the Attorney fees, and the court costs you can indeed get a felony charge expunged; however, that is not completely true. The definition of expunged means to obliterate or to remove completely. Therefore, having a charge expunged, within the meaning of the word, couldn't be further from the truth. As you can see, when a government entity tells you that you can get your criminal charge expunged from your record, they are not telling you the complete story. They are, once again, telling you a half-truth.

Even though it is true that a criminal charge and/or record can be removed from public viewing, the criminal record will still remain active within the government's internal records. Therefore, the criminal charge still remains; the court will only remove the felony charge from being accessed publicly. This means that a potential employer or anyone from the private sector will not have access to such an entry. Most of the American people are completely unaware that this type of procedure even exists. This brings us to the next question. If the government is willing to entertain the option for a felon to expunge their felony charge from the public record why isn't the charge removed as soon as they are released, especially when their punishment has been satisfied? Furthermore, why has the government agencies taken the liberty to make criminal records available to the public to begin with? If the person in question is so dangerous, then why release them? Yet again, this brings us to another question. At what point does the punishment for being convicted of a crime end? I ask this because when you are released, after satisfying your punishment, why is it that you are continually being punished thereafter in the form of a criminal record and, more importantly, with the removal of certain rights? If you take a closer look at the punishments that are being handed out, the purpose of putting you behind bars is to remove the majority of your freedoms, rights, and liberties. The punishment that had been handed down should have been sufficient, that's unless you have been deemed to be a risk or a threat to public safety, in which you should not have been released to begin with. If the mass majority of the American people believe that the answer is to continually punish someone even after they have fulfilled their obligations, then they actually believe in a false sense of security. Besides, this false sense of security and the unjust actions taken, in order to fulfill this misguided belief, have consequences attached to it. The way our "system", that's if we can call it a system, is currently being implemented today is that the misguided believers have purposely created scenarios that will increase the chances of repeat offenders. Due to this tactic, your taxes will rise in order to pay for the higher demand, as you have been doing so over the years. This means that not only are the criminals and the repeat offenders being punished, but the taxpayers are as well. One of the main reasons why there is so much confusion about this issue is because our legal system, unlike years ago, is being abused and misused. For the most part, this is true when a government agency punishes people unjustly in order to justify its own existence, keep you in the system in order to increase their revenue, and has plotted to remove your rights entirely. I know that sounds like a radical statement to make, but it's true nonetheless. Again, I say this because, when do the restrictions and the overall punishment ever end? For a convicted felon who happened to make a mistake, it doesn't end. This places the offender within the giant web of the legal system and of the law enforcement agencies' databases. This fact in itself proves that such a person will never again be entirely free. Being a convicted felon is a life sentence, unless a change is made. Don't get me wrong; I believe that there are certain individuals that need to be behind bars; however, today our system is only set up to address and deal with career criminals. It is in no way capable of dealing with the first-time offenders, which had made a mistake, or the individuals that have been charged with committing victimless crimes, which in itself is unacceptable.

If the American people do not address the injustices that are being perpetrated upon the American people you will wake up one day in a communist country. In return, you will find yourself without the freedoms, rights, and liberties that you had once enjoyed. I've said it before and I'll say it again. It is wrong for the governments of our country to believe that they can regulate limitations on the rights, liberties, and freedoms that the American people possess and then punish them for committing victimless crimes. To do so, is a criminal act in and of itself.

Your Signature

The Complete and Utter Disregard

This chapter may challenge the underlying foundation of what you may believe is our system of rules, equal justice, and what we fundamentally call "The United States of America". Despite the fact that you may have chosen to believe in what has become the current system, you have done so by ignoring all of the facts that surround you. The current system is no longer fair and honest, unlike years ago. Nonetheless, in order to establish the importance of this chapter, I must first ask you an important question. In doing so, you will need to answer the question honestly, as to what you truly believe. Do not supply a political answer that you may believe someone else would want to hear.

Are you ready?

Can anyone legally force you to agree to or sign a document or contract?

Did you answer no? If so, you're correct. You see it's quite simple. In a free country, the answer is indeed no! If, on the other hand, you had answered yes, then there can only be one of two circumstances or reasons as to why you would have supplied such an answer. You either didn't understand the question or, in fact, you believe in terrorism, extortion, and organized crime. This; however, is indicative to socialism, slavery, and a nation of injustices. Alternatively, for those of you that answered the question correctly, doesn't your answer contradict everything that we have been taught when it concerns the signing of tax returns, traffic tickets, the registration for Selective Service (which is the military draft documentation), the application for a Social Security Number, application for a Birth Certificate, and the application for a Marriage License? It most certainly does. Therefore, why is it that we have been told that we must fill out and sign these documents, which I refer to as "The Big Six"? Some would ask as to why I didn't add the driver's license to the list. I didn't add it to the list because most people already know and understand that obtaining a driver's license is completely voluntary. Think about it for a moment. More importantly, think about this. When it concerns your signature, why is it that you and almost every other American always over look the signing requirements of these 6 documents? You say you have no answer as to why? Well, you'll have one soon enough.

After giving it some thought, do you still believe that your signature belongs to you? Do you still believe that no one can force you to sign an agreement or document that you have not engaged in voluntarily? Do you believe that your signature has any significance whatsoever? If you had answered yes to all three, then why is it that most of the American population, outside of actually wanting a benefit, believe that they are required by law to fill out and sign these government documents, especially if you don't want to enter into such an agreement or obtain the benefit that is being offered? It is confusing to hear that the majority of people will agree that no one can force anyone to sign any document, but under their same breath they believe that they are required to sign the above six documents. Even though this is not true, there is an exception. I know that I have already covered this issue, but due to its importance I will cover it again. The exception is when you are voluntarily requesting such a benefit. Outside of that request, there is no lawful requirement mandating anything. The hidden truth about these 6 documents is that they are all indeed applications, just like the driver's license application. An application can never be mandatory, unless you are seeking a benefit. This detail may be hard for some people to comprehend; nonetheless all of these documents are applications. I say this because, no matter how you look at it, the 1040 "Income tax return" is an application as well. The 1040 tax return is a refund form only. It's an application for a refund, that's if the IRS believes you are entitled to one. It is not a document that assists you in paying a liability. For if it was, you would have used it throughout the year. Furthermore, the OMB[9] control number on the upper right hand corner of the form would be associated to a tax liability within the tax law. This, however, is not the case. As for obtaining a Social Security Number or Birth Certificate, I believe that both of these are self-explanatory. As you can see, the "SS-5 Application for a Social Security card" is self-explanatory. However, in spite of all the evidence, most of the American people, outside of certain groups like the Amish, still believe that they are required to obtain a Social Security Number. They also believe that they are required to fill out the IRS' documents and the application for the Social Security Administration, without being compensated for their time and labor for doing such. This defies logic, due to the fact that you must apply for such a refund and request such a number. If the law truly required everyone to fill out such a document then why is it that the Amish do not have to comply with this requirement? Besides, if this were truly a required act, the government agencies would be enforcing an unjust law, due to the fact that slavery and involuntary

---

[9] OMB – Office of Management and Budget is the largest office within the Executive Branch of the Federal government. The OMB oversees the federal budget; supervises the administration of Executive Branch agencies; and evaluates Executive agencies' programs, policies, and procedures. The OMB ensures that these agencies' policies and rules are consistent with the law and that of the Administrations policies.

servitude is illegal within our country. What does this mean? This means that you, as a living human being, have the right to choose to enter into an agreement or not. No one has the lawful authority to force you to agree to or enter into any agreement or contract, even though they may have offered to compensate you for doing such.

Nevertheless, this next piece of information should blow your mind. In lieu of using the words "application for release" or "Bond" in its title, when you sign a traffic citation you have in fact agreed to either pay the amount of money as it appears on the citation or personally appear in court. Contrary to popular belief, signing the citation is not an admission of guilt. In fact, when you sign the citation, that document becomes an enforceable bond agreement due to the fact that you have been accused of committing a crime; you have been placed under arrest, and have been released on your own recognizance. In turn, when you sign the citation you have legally agreed to the conditions of the bond. The bond is, in itself, an agreement. If you think that the citation is not a bond, which contains an agreement for your release, just tell the Law Enforcement Officer, the next time you encounter one, that you are not going to sign the citation and see what will happen. I do not recommend this action, but if you were to exercise your liberty to choose not to sign the citation I can almost guarantee that you will see the truth. I know that some people may have a hard time accepting this detail, but it's true nonetheless. This same concept is exactly how each and every bond functions when a person seeks to be released from jail, at least until their court date. When you sign a traffic citation you have legally and voluntarily agreed to the written application to be released on your own recognizance and not to be taken to jail. At that moment, the arresting Officer will either approve or disapprove your written request. Therefore, due to the importance of this situation and being able to show how the American people are being turned into criminals, I must elaborate further. If the arresting Officer has already handed over a citation, to the person in custody[10], then that arresting Officer has already determined, during their custodial interrogation, that he or she is going to release the person in question. If, on the other hand, you think that an arresting Officer will not withdraw the offer or disapprove an unsigned request to be released, then that shows that you have always signed the governments' traffic citations or, commonly known as, "tickets". The sad part about all of this is that most of the American people are unaware that they, by law and by legal definition, are under arrest at the moment the Officer initiates the stop. If, for any reason, you have any doubt as to this being true just ask the Law Enforcement Officer, during your next encounter with one, if you are free to go, after he or she has stopped you? If the Officer says, "No, you are not free to go, this is a traffic stop", then at that point you are under arrest[11]. However, upon you signing the citation, the Officer will release you on your own recognizance. Due to this fact, you were under arrest no matter if you want to believe it or not. The question that arises of whether you are under arrest does not depend on the legality of the stop, but rather if you have the ability to exercise your personal liberty and to go on your way as you see fit. Being placed in custody is the same thing as being placed under arrest. Therefore, when a Law Enforcement Officer tells you that you cannot leave because you are in custody, due to the traffic stop, that is nothing more than a polite way to inform you that you are officially under arrest. Again, if you do not believe this, find an honest Police Officer and ask him or her, they will tell you the truth. Furthermore, what if you did not want to sign the citation and, at the same time, did not want to go to jail? This is how most people feel when they have encountered this type

---

[10] Custody defined – "the detention of a person by virtue of lawful process or authority in exercise of the power to deprive a person of his or her liberty, an arrest or the taking of a person in legal care." Black's Law dictionary

[11] Arrest defined – "A seizure or forcible restraint. The taking or keeping of a person in custody by legal authority." Black's Law dictionary, seventh edition

of situation. Nonetheless, what if this was true and you decided to take the citation and not sign with your normal signature? What if you had scribbled something that was, in fact, not your signature? Would the Officer except it and let you go on your way? Absolutely they would.

In view of the facts so far, I would ask you to consider this. If government officials and employees believe that we are required to sign these particular documents, then they have in fact taken one of the following positions listed below.

1. According to Federal and local authorities, our signatures are in fact insignificant and meaningless and they view our signature as a measure of submission.

2. We are being lied to when it concerns these documents.

3. We are not truly free, as most of us would believe.

4. All of the above.

Which one do you think it is?

If, in spite of all the evidence so far, you still believe that you have a right not to sign a document, then take the next statement into consideration before you reach a conclusion. If you believe that you have the right to remain silent, which includes not signing your signature, and you were punished for invoking such a right, would prove that you do not have that right. Furthermore, if it were found that you were entitled to make use of such a right, then this would prove that you had been victimized by a criminal act. It really is that simple. In order to complete this synopsis, one has to recognize that if you are punished for exercising a right then you do not have that right, at least within the minds of the ones that are conducting the punishment. If you truly have any rights at all, you cannot be punished for the mere fact of exercising any one of them. In spite of government abuse, the governments of our country are authorized to remove certain rights from individuals that have actually committed a true crime, wherein they have caused a harm or injury to another person. For that reason, the American people should take a closer look as to why the arresting Officer will take you to jail, because you had decided not to sign the traffic citation or "ticket". The reason is clear. The people within government believe, you have committed a crime and refused to voluntarily sign the bond in order to be released. But wait a second! What crime did you actually commit? This is the question. Did you murder someone; conduct reckless endangerment, or commit theft? No, all you did was exceed the maximum speed limit by 9 miles an hour, may not have come to a complete stop at a stop sign, or had decided not to sign the citation. Oh my, these are indeed terrible crimes. Just in case you didn't already know, that was a little sarcasm.

The American people need to wake up and start questioning the actions taken by their public servants. We need to start holding government employees and officials accountable for their actions. Why do I say this? It's simple. To arrest someone, meaning to take someone's liberty and freedom away from him or her, when no criminal act had occurred is inherently a criminal act in itself. As for those of you who would disagree, I completely understand what your position is. You believe that the governments of our country can truly create a right out of two wrongs. If you claim to be a believer of this crazy idea, this would undoubtedly prove that you are incompetent of being able to make any rational decisions and that you are lacking any type of moral judgment. Therefore, it is an absurd idea or concept to believe. Anyhow, in order to correct this injustice, everyone must be aware of the truth. The truth is, in order for a crime to be committed there has to be an injured party or a person that was placed in danger. Therefore, who was injured or placed in danger as a result of you exceeding the speed limit by 9 miles an hour or something as simple as having a tag light out on your vehicle? I'll tell you. No one! For that reason, you're starting to see the importance of why you should know your rights.

In view of all the facts, I must pose the same question again. If no one can force you to sign a document, especially when you don't want to sign, why is it that most of the American people always overlook and ignore the so-called signing requirements of these six documents? Well, the reason why most of us have overlooked and ignored the signing requirements of these documents is due to the fact that we have been lied to about the true nature of these documents. And, most of the American people are too afraid of their own government to do anything about it. It's sad to see that most of the American people are afraid to question anything when it concerns issues of government. This is due to the people being concerned about the repercussions that may arise for questioning the government's "authority". If you have any uncertainty, just try questioning the authority of a self-centered and mindless Law Enforcement Officer and see what will happen. Finally, your signature either belongs to you or it doesn't! You either have the RIGHT not to sign or you don't! Besides, have you ever thought of what the purpose of your signature is, at least beyond its surface? Some would say that it is to give your approval. However, this answer is not true. Are we to believe that the only way we can give our approval is in the form of a signature? I know that I can give my approval verbally.

We have truly reached a sad day in our country when the people have become afraid of "their own" government. If it is true, that the people are now afraid, it would be due to the fact that the public servants are no longer behaving as such and are now acting like they are the Masters. They, the government employees and officials, are supposed to respect the people within the private sector, but yet they do not. Speaking as an authority on this issue, most of them don't respect one another; therefore, why would anyone expect them to respect the people within the private sector? Most, not all, of the government employees and officials have become so disrespectful that a socialistic mentality has surfaced and due to their weapons, manpower, and prisons they are now forcing us to play along with their deceptive game of enslaving our country. With that said, have you ever sat down with your friends and/or family members and played a board game, like Monopoly for example? If so, wouldn't the average person take the time to read the rules so that they would know how to play the game correctly? It is a fact that most people, that have agreed to play the game voluntarily, will read the rules. However, when it concerns the lives of the American people very few sit down and read the rules of their own game called "life". The rules of this game are the laws and their governing body, which is the supreme law of them all, The Constitution of the United States of America. I understand that you may believe that it is impossible for the average person to sit down and read all of the laws, let alone understand them. It is virtually impossible to do such. There isn't enough time in your life, with everything else that is taking place, for you to have the ability to read all of the laws and their implementing regulations. However, one would think that you would have at least taken the time to read and understand the laws that directly affect you and your fellow Americans on a daily basis. I agree that it may be difficult, due to the secret word game that the governments of our country have created. Furthermore, I can understand how one may become overwhelmed with the task of comprehending the laws and their implementing regulations, because it was difficult for me as well. Nonetheless, it's your duty to understand the laws and to correct the government when it has stepped outside of the confines of the Federal and State Constitutions. In doing so, only then can we ensure that our country will remain as free as possible. The easiest way to accomplish this is to use your common sense, surround yourself with like-minded individuals, and at least read the Constitution. Once you have done so, only then will you understand the truth concerning the legality of the unjust laws that are currently being put into practice. Just because the legislature has decided to pass a law does not necessarily mean that the newly introduced law meets that Constitutional requirements making it legal. Therefore, when you have taken an in-depth review of any given law, along with its proposed purpose, and were to identify certain inconsistencies with the Constitution; you would have to consider the possibility that there is a hidden agenda for its creation. If this were to be the case, it would be unlawful for the governments of our country to implement such a law. Take the TSA for example. Everything about this agency is unlawful.

At this point, you may be battling with your emotions. If so, I completely understand. I found myself having to battle with all the lies, inconsistencies, and contradictions that had been introduced to me years ago. I'll give you a good example of what I am referring to. Years ago, when I was a young adult and about to enter the work force, my father sat me down and explained to me that my signature is one of the most important possessions that I will ever own. He also taught me that if I were to find myself getting ready to sign an agreement or document that I should make sure I read everything, including the fine print. He also added, if I were to ever find myself not understanding an agreement or document that I should consider not signing it, until the understanding of such document had been achieved. Consequently, for years, I believed that no one could legally, meaning without violence, force me to sign any agreement or document. Needless to say, my understanding and beliefs as to what my signature signifies would be challenged to its very core. If you take the time to actually think about your signature and what it truly represents you will also find yourself questioning your underlying beliefs as well. Still, I want to give you a good example of the complete and utter disregard of a person's signature. Almost a year after I entered the work force, as a young adult, it had become apparent that I was to do "my" first tax return. Due to the fact that I had no idea how to complete such a document, I solicited my father's help. After my father and I had completed the tax return, I told my father that I did not fully understand the tax document. He told me to sign it anyway. I then informed my father that I was confused. He then asked, "Why are you confused?" I stated that what he is telling me now contradicts everything that he had taught me about my signature and as to when I should sign or not. Therefore, you can imagine as to why I was so confused to hear my father instruct me to sign the tax return, especially when I didn't understand it. Nonetheless, when I told my father that he was contradicting what he had taught me, concerning my signature, he became very upset and said, "Just sign it!" So, like everyone else, I swallowed my principles and signed the tax return without understanding it. As I was signing the tax document, I again glance at the title and thought to myself; what am I returning to the government? I also wondered if that was the reason why they had named the document a "Tax Return"? If you really think about it, you are not returning anything to the government. The government is returning money to you, that's if they believe you were entitled to it. This is one fact that proves that the 1040 Tax Return is an application for a refund. At that moment, I felt that something was extremely wrong and, more importantly, I felt betrayed. Not only did I feel a sense of betrayal from my father, but also from my own government and my fellow Americans. Why do I say this? Well, for one reason. I believed what my father had taught me about my signature and, more importantly, what he had taught me about my rights and liberties, all of which has not changed. This would also include the founding principles of what makes up The United States of America, which I still believe to this day. Therefore, I felt betrayed because the American people have allowed the governments of our country to go unchecked for many of years without any accountability for their actions. Furthermore, the American people have chosen to ignore the fact that the governments of our country have broken the laws that have been created to protect innocent people, which includes, but is not limited to, extorting money from the American people. Without any accountability, the governments of our country will continue to break not only the rule of common decency and that of civility, but actual laws themselves.

Even though all of this is true, I want you to know that it's more than just the illegal behavior and extortion practices that are being perpetrated by the governments, at all levels. They have deceived the American people by lying to us about the signing requirements of the six documents spoken of earlier. The Federal government knew that if they were to obtain popular approval concerning these six documents they would have to lie to the American people. Why do I make such a claim? Well, ask yourself this. Who, in their right mind, would agree to such a thing or would be willing to turn over their hard earned money and/or wealth to a government entity, without being justly compensated in return with something of value? That's why I have always asked my fellow Americans, what do you receive in return for the money you pay in "Income" taxes? The answer is nothing. Again, to clarify, I am not referring to excise taxes, which are sales taxes. I am only referring to Income taxes. Therefore, the income tax within the U.S., as in many other socialist countries, is nothing more than a form of redistribution of wealth, which in the U.S. is illegal. The problem is that most people believe, due to the government's unrelenting propaganda, that they are required to fill out and sign government documents, even though they are not requesting nor do they want any benefit from government. The solution is to become aware of the actual legal requirements of said documents and educate yourself, your friends, and your family members on the rights and liberties that you as Americans are entitled to. In addition, every American, like yourself, needs to stop believing what is told to you by the government and start questioning everything. Remember, the Freedom of choice is the essence of liberty. Therefore, we must stand together in order to restore our liberty and return government back to its proper role.

Marriage Is Sacred

Out of all the personal contracts that have ever existed in this world, the marriage between two people is, by far, the most sacred agreement that anyone could ever enter into. A marriage is not only the most sacred of all the agreements; it is one of the most significant and fundamental liberties and/or rights that we, as human beings, possess. If you noticed, I did not say the ability to enter into a marriage is a privilege. It is inherently a right held by every person. The freedom to enter into the contract of marriage is protected by the Constitution under Article I, Section 10, which states as follow:

> "No State shall ... make any ... Law impairing the Obligation of Contracts."

As you can see, it's not a special benefit that's only enjoyed by a few, which is the nature of a privilege. Furthermore, when two people have decided to become life partners, once the offer of marriage has been presented and an acceptance has been received, they have at that point become married. There is no legal requirement to proclaim your marriage publicly; however, if you want to announce your declarations publicly by way of a ceremony that's up to you to decide. Either way, the lack of a marriage license and a public ceremony does not negate the fact that, once the offer has been presented and the acceptance was received, the couple has entered into the agreement of marriage. A marriage agreement is legally and widely accepted as a verbal contract between two people. Just because, for the most part, the agreement may not be in a written form does not discredit the marriage nor does it relieve any one of the partners of their obligations that they had voluntarily entered into. If you and your partner agreed to enter into the agreement of marriage, other than asking your partner's parents for their blessings, there is no other person or entity that should be involved in your decision or allowed to have the ability to hinder such an agreement. Again, if two people claim that they have exchanged marital vows, even though there was no additional witnesses at the time the agreement took place, the marriage must be recognized and accepted as a valid marriage. One of the major misconceptions that we are led to believe is that the two people who have decided to exchange vows are not to be considered as witnesses. This couldn't be further from the truth. Just like in any other agreement or contract, the first two witnesses are always the two people that have chosen to enter into such an agreement. Therefore, there is no mandate that there be any more than two to three witnesses that should participate in any given marriage. As stated before, the first two witnesses are the two people that have actually consented to becoming life partners and the third witness is God. Other witnesses are not required in any way; however, they are inevitable due to the fact that you and your partner will continually introduce yourselves to your friends, family members, and acquaintances as a married couple. Consequently, once you have done so, the people privileged to that introduction have at that point become an additional witness to your marriage. This is due to the fact that you and your partner have openly and publicly made additional declarations of your marriage. Just because a person was unable to be present for the initial ceremony does not in any way nullify the marriage. It hurts me to see that most of the American people have been tricked into believing so many lies. What lies am I referring to? Well, get ready. I am going to reveal a secret concerning the marriage license, which the governments of our country do not want you to know. No government, here in the U.S., has the authority to mandate that you obtain such a license. The government only has the legal authority to require the church, which has been incorporated; to mandate that such a marriage license be present before the Pastor can conduct the ceremony. This is due to the fact the churches have voluntarily incorporated their establishments and have obtained a tax exemption status, which grants the government the authority to mandate certain aspects of the church's operations. This defies the principles of the separation between Church and State. Some people immediately disagree when such a statement is made. However, these are the same people that claim to believe that they have a right to enter into a marriage without being required to obtain permission, but at the same time believe that they are required to obtain a marriage license in order to become married. How absurd is that?

Over the last 85 years, the governments of our country have once again fooled most of the American people into believing that they do not have the right, liberty, or freedom to enter into a marriage without the government's permission, by way of a license. It is unfortunate that most of the American people are convinced that they must obtain the government's permission in order to enter into a marriage with another. This is flat out ridiculous and deceitful. The deception; however, is not limited to the State and Federal governments. This deception includes most, if not all, of the churches being misled into believing that they also have a requirement to register their churches as 501(c)(3) tax-exempt religious organizations. Again, this couldn't be further from the truth. The Federal government, along with certain politicians like President Lyndon B. Johnson, offered the churches certain benefits if they were to register their church organizations with the government. These benefits came with stipulations, acting more like handcuffs and shackles rather than true benefits. The Federal government's intent was to silence the church and to prohibit them from addressing certain issues that the American people believed to be vitally important to their rights and liberties. The tax exemption, which the churches sought after, has had a terrorizing effect upon the right to free speech within the churches. The State and Federal governments were surprised to see how easy it was to swindle the clergy into believing that they needed a benefit, especially when the churches already enjoyed the same benefit that was being offered. The benefit that was being offered, by the State and Federal governments, was a tax exemption for their church organizations, once they incorporated their churches. The truth of the matter is that churches were never taxable nor were they required to incorporate their establishments. The fact is the churches were to remain separate from all of the State governments, as according to the law. If you were to take the time to research this fact you would see that the law has not been changed. Therefore, why would the State and Federal governments want the churches to become incorporated? Well, in order for a church to be taxable it must first fall under the jurisdiction of the taxing authority of the government. One of the underlying principles behind the "Separation between the Church and State Clause" is so that the churches would never fall under the jurisdiction of any government. This was to ensure that the churches would remain free to practice their religion openly and without any restrictions from government. The law has always placed the churches outside of the jurisdiction of both the Federal and State governments. The Law states as follows:

> *"Congress shall make no law respecting an establishment of religion, or prohibiting the free exercise thereof; or abridging the freedom of speech..."*

Furthermore, the United States Code Title 26, along with IRS publication 557, state that church organizations, *"are exempt automatically"*. Therefore, if the churches had not fallen into the trap of incorporating and filing an IRS document, making the church a tax-exempt organization, the churches would have never needed an exemption status nor would they have fallen under the government's jurisdiction. Why do I say this? Well, the Law specifically states that Congress has no authority to create any law when it concerns churches. The Law never intended to exempt the church; it was written to show that the tax law never applied to the churches to begin with. Yes, there is a difference between something not applying to you and that of you being exempt from that same requirement. You cannot be exempt from something that does not apply to you. It must first apply in order for you to be exempt from its requirements. Knowing the churches are not taxable in the first place, why did the churches seek permission to be tax-exempt? It's all due to the ignorance of the clergy, the collective mentality of the people, and the misguided advice from the so-called professional Attorneys and CPAs. I am tired of hearing the excuses that "we didn't know", "everyone else has done it", or "our Attorney told us that we had to do it". That is no excuse! It's up to you to know your rights and the Law itself. If you do not take the time to know and understand your rights, how can you expect to have any? There is no reason why you shouldn't know the rules to the game that everyone in America is participating in. Again, the rules I am referring to consist of the laws of both the State and Federal government, including the U.S. Constitution. You're probably saying to yourself, "I don't have the time". Well, do you really think that the governments of our country will not take advantage of you for the mere fact that you do not know what your rights and liberties consist of? Believe me, they will. There are extreme consequences for not knowing what is required or not required of you. More importantly, there are dire consequences for not knowing what your rights and liberties consist of, all of which has been secured by the Law. The consequences that will follow, due to the majority of people not knowing what their rights consist of, is that the government, along with other players in this game, will trample upon the rights and liberties of others within our country. All the same, I have digressed.

Have we finally reached a point in time where stupidity and complacency has replaced logical reasoning? I say this because it appears to be true. It repulses me to be part of this now socialistic system of lies. Furthermore, I'm going to make what may seem to be to some people a radical statement, but true nonetheless. All of the 50 States have, in their own minds, made a marriage between two people illegal. How do I know this, you may be asking yourself? If the governments of our country, along with the churches themselves, are instructing us that we must have a license in order to get married, then all one has to do is research the definition of what a license is. A license is nothing more than a revocable document issued by a government entity granting you the authority to do a specific thing that would otherwise be illegal to do without such license. So, with that said, we must acknowledge that the States, along with the Federal government, has truly made marriage illegal. That is, unless you have their permission. This also applies to everything else that has been regulated as a licensed activity. For example, they are licensing the inherent right to use and operate "your own" personal property, like that of your automobile. The government is also regulating and licensing other inherent rights such as; the right to carry a firearm, the right to work, open a business, and the fundamental right to construct a home. The authority to license implies, by its nature, the power to prohibit. However, this chapter is specifically on the marriage license; therefore, let's continue with such.

Just incase you are not aware of the origin of the marriage license and the reason or reasons as to why the State governments have implemented such a license, I'll address it now. It all took place during the 19th century when certain people wanted to marry someone of a different ethnic background. Marrying interracially was completely unacceptable during those years and, in some ways, it is still frowned upon. Nonetheless, this does not justify making the marriage between two people illegal. The State governments were in fact using the prohibitive nature of the license in order to deny some people the right to enter into a marriage. During the mid-to-late 1800's, the marriage licensing requirements only applied to interracial couples. Consequently, the people of different ethnic backgrounds were required to apply for and obtain a marriage license. As for obtaining one, that's a completely different story and was all decided by the local governments. That's until the Federal government noticed that they could get involved in the action. During the year of 1923, the Federal government passed the Uniform Marriage and Marriage-Licensing Act. Soon, thereafter, the Federal government established the Uniform Marriage and Divorce Act. It wasn't until six years later, during 1929, that the Federal government mandated that the States follow suit. Therefore, between the years of 1929 and that of 1930, every State had adopted some type of marriage licensing law, which on its surface may seem to require everyone to obtain such a license before his or her marriage would become recognizable. Again, that couldn't be further from the truth. The dreadful part about the Uniform Marriage and Divorce Act is that they were anticipating a lot of divorces. As a result, the government's legal system was anticipating a new source of revenue. Why do I say that? For crying out loud, they use the word divorce in its title.

Now, I am aware that some people may become upset at this point and that you may be one of them. If so, calm down. The reason why you may have become upset is due to the fact that you were required to obtain a marriage license when you and your spouse had decided to enter into the agreement of marriage. If I am correct, this is no reason to become upset. You should be upset at yourself for not researching and knowing the truth about the application of a marriage license. You're probably saying to yourself, everyone is required to get one. This, again, is not true. Do you think the Amish have used a government document to ensure that outsiders, like the governments of our country, will recognize their marriages? No, they do not. They don't want anything from their local and Federal government, other than to be left alone. Do you believe that the Amish have the right to be left alone? Yes, they do. Well, guess what? So do we, the American people. To be left alone, without government involvement in your everyday life, is one of the purposes of the Federal and State Constitutions. Again, for informational purposes, the Law does not require you to obtain a license in order to enter into the agreement of marriage. The law only requires the churches, which have been incorporated by way of a State charter, to obtain a marriage license from you before they can conduct the wedding. What does this mean? Again, this means that the churches have voluntarily put themselves under the government's jurisdiction and are now required to follow suit. Why is that? Again, most of the churches have been fooled into believing that they were required to incorporate their establishments and obtain a tax exemption, which I spoke of earlier. In doing so, they have been mandated, by the government, to required marriage licenses from the people seeking to become married. If a church has decided to incorporate, by way of a State Charter and obtain the 501(c)(3) tax exemption from the IRS, they now fall under the rules and procedures of the government. Therefore, all corporations are a creation of the State, which places them under the authority of the State government. You; however, are not required to follow this requirement, because you have not incorporated yourself, which would place you under this authority. Here's a thought, what if we have been incorporated? If we have been fooled into becoming our own personal corporations, we would have done so foolishly by obtaining a birth certificate and Social Security Number. The birth certificate is proof of the corporate charter and the Social Security

Number is proof of the tax ID number, which all corporate entities are required to have. Nevertheless, these facts give a person something to think about.

What has transpired over the years is the governments of our country have started to intrude into the lives of the American people, by unjustly implementing unlawful and illusionary regulations and licensing requirements. It is unbelievable for the people within government to believe that they have the authority to negate the rights of the American people. This includes something as simple as prohibiting the people from entering into the agreement of marriage, at least without their permission. According to Federal and State records, their justification to involve themselves within the marriages of the American people is due to the interest of the social welfare, to protect the people from disease, to ensure that inappropriate marriages were not to take place; to ensure accurate State records; and to ensure the people had adequate time to think about the commitment that they were about to enter into. Let's make it perfectly clear; no government has the authority to negate any right, let alone a right that has been specifically protected by the Constitution, unless you have been convicted of committing a crime. What has happened to our country? Have we become so brainwashed into believing that we are the government's servants and, in turn, have resorted to giving the people within government complete control over our lives, including our marriages? This is completely ludicrous, especially when they pass laws that deliver a false sense of security. Still, let's take a moment and address some of the reasons as to why the governments believe that they have the need to involve themselves within our marriages. Some of their reasons, as noted earlier, consist of the interest in the social welfare, protecting the public from disease, and setting a grace period to prevent stupidity from occurring. In view of these, let me address each separately. The first is the interest in the social welfare. What does this mean? This was deliberately written vague so that the governments of our country could justify their authority to enforce these newly proposed laws, like those that address marriages and divorces. This is nothing more than an excuse to justify the expansion of government within these areas, which grants the local governments the authority to oversee the settlements of divorce. Outside of collecting a tax in the form of a marriage-licensing fee and increasing revenues within the legal system, the primary reason why the governments have made the attempt to govern other people's marriages is to exploit the incompetence of the American people by charging them for the adjudication of their marital matters. Nevertheless, most people, due to their shortsightedness and lack of education, have turned to the government by way of the marriage license in order to secure, by force if necessary, their personal interests within their marriages. All one has to do in order to secure their marital interest is to create a written contract. This can be accomplished with the help of an Attorney. Sadly enough, most people do not seek the assistance of an Attorney to create the agreement of marriage; they only seek such assistance in order to protect property that they believe belongs to them. This can be proven by the fact that prenuptial agreements are being used. This is becoming a common occurrence due to the fact that certain individuals are experiencing reservations and/or trust issues within their relationship. Therefore, why would anyone enter into a marriage knowing that they have doubts or trust issues with their potential partner? Still, making a government entity a third party to your marriage is not the answer. This only grants the government the authority to mandate the outcome of a dispute, no matter if you had agreed to the conditions or not.

If only the American people had been informed of the truth, concerning government marriages by way of a marriage license, they would have had the fortitude to stay away from the government license and would have secure their interests with a personal contract. This; however, would not have been a concern for government involvement if it were not for the people being taught that selfishness and shortsightedness is okay. If it were not for this type of behavior and mindset, the majority of people would have taken the time to get to know their potential partner, before the thought of marriage would ever cross their minds. Therefore, no one should substitute a private agreement, which requires full disclosure, for that of a governmental contract, which is created when the marriage license is used. Again, the marriage license legally makes the government a third party to your marriage and automatically grants the government the authority to create the terms of your marital agreement and to be the arbitrator thereto. This is especially true when it concerns the dissolution of a marriage, if such a separation were to occur. How unfair is that? Why would I make such a claim? I do so, for one main reason. The terms of the agreement are not disclosed and; therefore, you are not fully aware of what you are about to enter into. For if you had been informed, you might not have entered into such an agreement. Basically, you have entered into an agreement without fully understanding the terms.   Moreover, the terms of your marital agreement are created and decided by the State governments, not you.   More importantly, the terms created by these governments change from time to time and from State to State, which defies a legal standard that requires full disclosure of all agreements.   If certain information has been withheld from you, how can you make a fully informed decision? It's simple, you can't. In the absence of a marital contract and full disclosure, how can anyone know what the government is going to mandate or require a person to agree to, when it concerns the matters of a divorce?   The parties to a government marriage, which was created when a marriage license was obtained, are at the mercy of the government and their courts. For instance, if a Judge were to order you to pay an amount of money or to continue the payments on a home that you are no longer allowed to live in, how would you feel? Furthermore, when did you agree to such an arrangement? It's simple, you had not agreed to such an absurdity. Believe it or not, these situations occur more than you may believe. The sad and inevitable part is that in most of the separations that occur today is when someone uses the force of government to obtain property from another that is in no way justified, but rather designated as an entitlement. With that said, the force of government should never be used in place of common decency, a private contract, and, more importantly, civility. Some people disagree and continue to believe in these so-called entitlements. Please forgive me when I say that this mostly applies to women. Therefore, when they are asked as to why they would believe in such a process, most reply with, "My feelings were hurt and I want to take him for everything he has." I couldn't believe what I was hearing! Just because your feelings were hurt or you believe that you are entitled to someone else's property does not justify the use of government force, without first proving the contractual obligations. Apparently, most people, when it concerns their emotional mindset, have not heard of cutting their losses and walking away.

The second reason that is given to justify government marriage licenses is to protect the public from disease. This is completely preposterous. Are we to believe that a marriage license, a piece of paper, is going to prevent sexual transmitted diseases from occurring between two consenting adults? If, on the other hand, you actually believe that a piece of paper is going to prevent two people from having sexual relations, then why is it that fornication and teenage pregnancies exist today? That's because a piece of paper, like that of the marriage license, cannot prevent anything. For if it could, there would be no divorce. In any case, let's move on to the next issue of inappropriate marriages. What gives the government or anyone for that matter the authority or right to determine what is or what is not socially acceptable as a marriage? I have the answer to this question. No one! At least no one other than the two people that are about to enter into the agreement of marriage, period! Finally, let's address the last concern. This is where some States have required a grace or waiting period from the issuance of the marriage license to the date that the ceremony can be conducted. The reason behind this requirement is to ensure that the parties involved have carefully thought about their potential commitment. It is ridiculous to even fathom that the governments of our country have taken an active role in regulating limitations on freedoms, contractual provisions, and that of stupidity. It is absurd to believe that government has this authority.

With that said, what did people do before marriage licenses? Did the people of years past not get married, due to the fact that marriage licenses did not exist? That question may sound silly, but it's still a legitimate question nonetheless. The truth is that marriage licenses have not always been around and the American people have always had the freedom to enter into the agreement of marriage, without the involvement of a government entity or a marriage license. The Amish know this to be true and; therefore, they understand the importance of keeping the government out of their marriages. Interestingly enough, the governments have not only made a marriage between two people illegal, by implementing a license, they have also made unwarranted divorces somehow widely acceptable, which is morally wrong outside of betrayal, like that of adultery. In my humble opinion, most people decide to get married because they know they have a way out, the divorce. This is due to the government creating immoral laws. Still, if you decide to get a divorce, the State government will surely screw you in the end. One of the simplest steps that can be taken to secure our wealth and freedom is to stop making the governments of our country a party to our personal contracts. One of the reasons why "our" judicial system was created is to litigate our differences within our contractual obligations, which we have chosen to voluntarily enter into. The government should only be used as a neutral party in litigating differences brought forth before them. The government should never be used as an authority to resolve differences concerning their rules and/or conditions. Besides, if you and your partner truly love and trust one another, why would you care if the governments of our country recognize your marriage or not? I have asked this question a lot. The most common answer I receive as to why anyone would want to obtain a marriage license, outside of imitating what others have done, is that they want their marriage to be legal. What they actually mean, when confronted, is that they want their marriage to be legally enforceable. What they do not understand is that all contracts, containing proper consideration, are legal and are legally enforceable. Therefore, with this knowledge, I was able to formulate a conclusion as to why the American people are foolishly obtaining marriage licenses. The conclusion consists of three parts. The first is that most of the American people are ignorant when it concerns their rights, liberties, and freedoms. The second consists of them being able, in the case of a separation, to use the force of government to unwarrantedly retaliate against their former spouse, due to their self-centered, selfish, and misguided anger or misplaced trust. The third is that they believe they can force their will upon others, like that of private business owners. They believe that a government "backed" marriage gives them the ability to force insurance companies, employers, and financial institutions to conduct business with them as a married couple, all with the threat of government intervention. This type of mentality is communistic in nature and is morally wrong. We don't need criminals in the form of government employees or officials to address what the free market will adapt to. Therefore, you need to research how you can secure your interest in any contract, including the agreement of marriage. Here's a hint. Affidavits, contracts, and witnesses work well. Stand up for your contractual rights and stop allowing the governments of our country from enticing you into waiving your rights just because they offer you a benefit, which in the end acts more like handcuffs and shackles rather than a true benefit. Basically, stop being a slave to the government and start standing up for your rights, liberties, and freedoms. For if you do not, a socialistic mentality will prevail, which always leads to collectivism and then, ultimately, to communism! This, unfortunately, is where the United States of America is headed.

A Man's Home Is His Castle

Throughout American history, everyone knew that each and every person had the opportunity to own land in the same manner as the King of England. Therefore, once a person had chosen to acquire land, it was understood that he or she owned their land completely and without any restrictions, which included the right to defend their property at all costs. That is, unless they had voluntarily waived their rights to such ownership by way of a contractual obligation. In absence of such a contract, all of the American people held absolute title to their land. Unfortunately, somewhere over the last 100 years, the American people have forgotten this. The consequence of not knowing the past and the Law itself is that we were tricked into becoming a nation of modern day serfs. This; however, was never the intent of our country. This is especially sad since we were once the land of Kings. The ability to own property, as a King, and to have limited government, with secured rights, liberties, and freedoms, one would have to agree that this is truly "The American Dream". With that said, one needs to recognize that the American Dream, that I am referring to, consists of different aspects. The most important characteristic that would apply to the American people is the ability to own property, personal or otherwise. Over the years, I have noticed that most of the American people are completely ignorant to the principles of what constitutes property ownership. They have no idea as to what the ownership of property entails and, more importantly, what is required of said ownership. The ability to own property is the essence of liberty and freedom. Today, some would say that buying a home is the biggest "investment" that you'll ever make. I on the other hand disagree, due to the circumstances that have arisen today. If you decide to purchase a home, you will more than likely have to finance it through a financial institution and will have to work for many years in order to pay off that "investment". This type of purchase sounds more like a liability as opposed to an investment, which contradicts what most people believe. Still, it's quite simple. An investment puts money in your pocket and a liability takes money out of your pocket. Therefore, so long as you live within your home it is a liability. Only when it is sold for a profit or passed down to your children will it become an investment, but not before. Nevertheless, lets continue.

One should remember that the phrase "A Man's Home Is His Castle" is one of the primary reasons why this country was originally founded, outside of the lack of freedom and high taxes. If you think about it, that sounds familiar. Doesn't it? Nevertheless, the American people had fought for the status to be their own sovereign, the supreme authority, over their land and property. This country was established to fulfill that intent. Essentially, the American people wanted to get away from the concept of having a King. They, in turn, had the idea that the people within the United States of America could be free and govern themselves. The American people believed that they should also have the right to own property in the same manner as the King of England. What a radical idea, huh? However, I must point out that their idea, due to the fact that they had implemented it, is the reason why the United

States of America exists today. Nonetheless, this is where the concept of "A Man's Home Is His Castle" came from. The reason behind this saying is that, as Americans, we have the right to do whatever we want with our property and to defend our castles if necessary. Obviously, this is the way it's supposed to be in America, the land of the free, but it is not. Somewhere along the way it has changed.

During my childhood, I was told over and over again that a man's home is his castle and as to what it meant. I remember during a family gathering, in the early 1980's, my father and uncle were talking about this very issue. They were talking about the ownership of their homes and as to what they were allowed to do on their property. During the 1960's and 70's, an owner of a single-family home was able to build a tree house for their children, put a shed on their property, and even build a fence around their property, all without any restrictions. As the years passed, I noticed something inconsistent with what I had been taught, concerning the ownership of property. What I noticed is when a neighbor of ours had talked about putting a pre-built shed on their property, one of two phrases kept coming up. The phrases were, "Do I need a permit...?" or "You need a permit...!" I kept asking myself, why is that we are required to ask for permission to put something as simple as a pre-built shed on our land, if we were indeed the rightful owners of our property? It's simple; we shouldn't be required to ask for permission. However, due to safety reasons, I understand why certain inspections and permits are required on public property. As a result, do you believe we should be required to ask for permission when it concerns our private property, especially if we do not belong to a HOA (Home Owners Association)? It is ridiculous to believe that we, the property owners, are required to asked for permission, pay a permit fee, and pay a recurring property tax year after year in order to use our own property. Again, it is completely illogical to think that a person has to spend more of their wealth just for the mere fact of owning their own property. I thought that property ownership was an investment and; furthermore, a right. When did it become a privilege and, more importantly, a way to extract the wealth from the American people? The right to ownership should allow you the opportunity to create wealth, which gives you the ability to save for you and your families' future. The evidence that home ownership is no longer an investment has always been in plain sight. Between the financial institutions, due to the interest being paid, and the government agencies, due to the payment of property taxes, should prove such a statement to be true. These entities are extracting a good portion of your wealth, all for the mere fact of you exercising your right of ownership, which is absurd. Today, the average American, even if they own property, has a hard time creating any type of wealth; therefore, this should tell us one thing. We are not the legal and absolute owners of our property and that there is another interested party at play here. For this reason, I had to do some research on this issue. What had become apparent to me, during my research, is that we are not the absolute owner of our property and someone or some entity was extracting our wealth through fraud and extortion.

Due to the inspiration of wanting to know the truth, I enthusiastically researched this issue and what I found is interesting to say the least. Simply put, there are three types of property ownership that exist in the United States and they consist of the legal, equitable, and the absolute owners. However, today, there are only two basic types of titles that are being used to secure property ownership within the United States. They are the Fee Simple[12] and Allodial titles. Let me address both of these. The first is the Fee

---

[12] Fee Simple as – "An interest in land that, being the broadest property interest allowed by law…" "[Fee Simple] is a term not likely to be found in modern conversation between laymen…" "Yet to a layman… …it refers to the elementary social relationship of feudalism… …the words 'fee' and 'feudal' are closely related…" *Black's Law Dictionary*.

Simple title. Fee Simple title means, in simple terms, that you can maintain limited and restricted rights to the property, which includes, but is not limited to, being able to occupy the property and sell your interests at any time, all for a simple fee. This simple fee is identified as a recurring property tax that is assessed year after year. The Fee Simple title, when it applies to the people in the private sector, only grants equitable ownership in the property and the legal ownership is granted and/or retained by the Cities, Counties, or State governments. This is evidenced by the existence of property taxes. That's why there is a thing called a bundle of rights, which is transferred to the person buying such property versus having the all-inclusive rights transferred to the new purchaser. As for the second, Allodial[13] title or Allodial Ownership means absolute ownership, where you have been granted both legal and equitable ownership, unlike Fee Simple. Therefore, Allodial title transfers all of the rights to the property. Today, however, the majority of people are only using one type of property ownership and that is the equitable ownership conveyed by the Fee Simple title. This applies when the property has been registered or recorded on public land records. If you were to look at your deed or mortgage you'll see that you own your property in Fee Simple. Furthermore, due to the recordation of your deed onto public land records, you have lost certain rights that are inherent to absolute ownership. You being required to obtain a permit in order to get permission to add an extension, a shed, or even a driveway to your home demonstrates that such a statement is true. Moreover, this is also proven by the payment of property taxes. Therefore, if you are required to do any of the above, how are you the complete owner of the property? It's

---

[13] Allodial Title Defined – *Black's Law Dictionary* – "Allodial title is a concept in some systems of property law. It describes a situation where real property is owned free and clear of any encumbrances, including liens, mortgages and tax obligations. Allodial title is inalienable, in that it cannot be taken by any operation of law for any reason whatsoever."

simple; you're not. Any logical person would have to agree. Just in case you disagree, do you recall this old saying? If it walks like a duck, quacks like a duck, and looks like a duck, then it's a duck? Therefore, the duck here is that we are not the absolute owners of our property. Someone else has an interest in "our" property and they are stealing our wealth, all within plain sight. Can you guess who it is? If not, you will soon be made aware.

An important point to remember is that all direct taxes, such as property and income taxes, are theft no matter how you look at it. Theft is defined as obtaining someone else's property through coercion, threats, and ultimately the use of force. If you think that coercion, force, and the threat of violence are not being used today, then you do not believe that government will use these tactics in the collection of taxes. If this is the case, I only have one thing to say. Stop paying your Property and/or Income Taxes and see what will happen to you. Yes, I know. You will not see any force or violence at first. It will all start with you receiving a few letters asking you why you haven't paid. Moreover, if you are unable to or have chosen not to pay the government's extortion fee, their tactics of force and violence will certainly emerge. Your property will be taken away, by force if necessary, and you could possibly face jail or prison time, all because you could not pay or have chosen to protect your rights, liberties, and freedom. This is why the founders made direct taxation illegal, unless in time of war. The sad part about all of this, outside of dealing with a government entity that believes your property and labor belongs to them, is that they will brake into your home and seize any and all of your assets. Make no mistake, this will happen. Furthermore, if you decide to defend yourself and your family, they will kill you. If this isn't force and violence then I don't know what is.

By not correcting these injustices, we have allowed the governments of our country the ability to start enslaving the American people, which was intended to turn the free and successful Americans into serfs. I don't know about you, but I will not stand for the governments treating us as serfs. I will not allow my fellow Americans to be treated as a person that is in a condition of servitude, which requires them to render their services to the government. The governments of our country are not our lords or superiors. To the contrary, we are the Masters over our governments, both federally and locally! There is, however, a reason why the Bankers and certain government officials would like us to believe that we are Surfs. Some people would have a need to ask why. Again, it's quite simple. A Serf, of years past, was allowed to occupy and work the land owned by such a lord or superior; however, the Serf is required to pay the lord or superior a simple fee to do such, that's why we have Fee Simple titles. Does this sound familiar as to what is happening today? What's even sadder is that some of my fellow Americans, who happen to be Attorneys and/or Real Estate Brokers, seem to believe and continue to make one of the most contradicting statements that I have ever heard, concerning a position on what Fee Simple title truly means. They state that the Fee Simple title or ownership represents absolute ownership of real property, which couldn't be further from the truth. This is proven within their own statement. As they try to justify their misconception of what the Fee Simple title truly conveys, they continue on by stating; that while Fee Simple ownership is limited to four basic government powers like that of taxation, eminent domain, police powers, and where property is reverted to the State in the absence of legal heirs, they still believe the Fee Simple title conveys absolute ownership. It really is quite simple. They are either completely brainwashed or they are simply repeating what they have been taught. I have asked myself; are they hearing the crap they are shoveling? As they understand it, the American people are limited in their ownership, due to the powers of government. Isn't that what I just said? Furthermore, how is it that the government gains these powers? Could it be through the use of the Fee Simple title? You bet it does. More importantly, some go on to claim that this has taken place due to the fact that we have shifted from Allodial title to the title of Fee Simple. You have to be kidding me; didn't I just say the same thing? What in the world are these so-called professionals trying to accomplish, by stating such a contradicting statement? As I see it, it's nothing more than double talk, which has been designed to confuse the average person. This is especially true when they claim that the Fee Simple title conveys absolute ownership when, in fact, it does not. It is; therefore, a huge contradiction and I am blown away that these intelligent people would believe such a lie.

If we were to take another look at the definition of what a Serf is, you will come to a conclusion that this definition is currently identifying the majority of the American people. What is so disheartening is that the intent of our country was to ensure that the American people would retain their position of master and that the governments of our country would remain the servants; however, as you can see, the roles have changed. Still, why would the American people allow this to happen? Despite the true intent of our country, we have allowed our country to become a virtual feudal[14] society, were land is held with a condition of a fee. This system of land ownership has made the Federal, State, and local governments the "King". Again, to prove this, can the governments of our country, just like a King, take your property for failing to pay their extortion fees? Apparently, the answer is yes. This proves that we are no longer living in a free society, but rather a socialistic system, which is currently bordering a communistic way of life here in America. Some people reject these facts without researching them, which is sad to say the least. However, I know that some people believe that property taxes are needed to pay for schools and whatever the

---

[14] Feudal Defined – *Black's Law Dictionary* – "1. A landholding system, particularly applying to medieval Europe, in which all are bound by their obligations to pay a fee for their land ownership to a Lord or King. The lord was obligated to give the vassal [tenant] some land, protection.

government says they need it for. However, isn't there another way to pay for these so-called government services, without us being threatened that our property will be taken from us? Yes, there is. It's called sales taxes. I suggest that we only allow governments the ability to operate on indirect taxes, as the founders had sought to achieve. Why would I suggest such a thing? It would require the governments to satisfy their customers, the American people. If the governments were failing to satisfy their customers, you and I could choose to not be a repeat customer. This is exactly how the free market works. Furthermore, this would also protect our property from the government mafia and their loan sharking tactics. The American people are now aware that the government believes that you have taken out a loan with them when they claim you owe back taxes. This is proven by the penalties and interest they are charging the American people. The amount of penalties and interest the government has decided to charge is terrifyingly similar to that of the illegal amounts charged by the crime families of years past. An interesting point that everyone should take into consideration, is when your property has been seized, you are not compensated for the remaining equity in said property. You will lose the entire value of "your" home, especially if it goes to auction and sells for a lot less than it's worth on the open market. Even though you may have had a tremendous amount of equity, you will not be compensated for that value. Now that you know the truth, how can a person claim to be the absolute owner of their property, if they hold title to it in the form of Fee Simple? It's simple, they can't! Unfortunately, some people find this to be an upsetting topic. Still, it is too important to ignore any longer. All I have asked of you is that you keep an open mind and it is apparent that you have done so, since you have made it this far. I thank you for that.

Even though there are other ways to hold title to property, the people within the County, State, and Federal governments have chosen to only accept, for recordation purposes, the title of Fee Simple. I wonder why? The deceptive part to all of this, as you have become aware, is that this type of title only conveys one of the two aspects of absolute ownership. It does not convey, as most lawyers and real estate agents would believe, the aspects of being the legal and equitable owner. This is proven by the fact the government has assigned a Trustee to over see their legal interest in "your" property. Most people are not aware of how the government gained the legal aspect of the absolute ownership. They had done so for the mere fact that a financial institution had collateralized the property and the deed to said property had been recorded on their public land records. Most people believe that the public land records exist so that the public at large can record their land contracts, which will make known to the public their ownership. Even though there is some truth to this claim that is not the only thing that is being accomplished by recording your property on public land records. The truth is that your private property, according to the law, has become public property and/or land, as noted by its recordation on PUBLIC LAND RECORDS. That's what gives the government the authority and jurisdiction to tax "your" property, mandate that you pay, and grants them the authority to seize "your" property for failing to do so. This would also include their destructive tactics of eminent domain[15], wherein they will take "your" property for whatever reason they see fit. There would be no issue of eminent domain abuse if the American people would have kept their contracts private or just simply recorded their agreements and/or contracts on Public Record, not on the Public Land Records. Why does everyone believe that they are required to record their private contracts of land purchases or the Deeds to said property on Public LAND Records? The Public Records Division only makes the documents that had been recorded available for public viewing; however, by recording private Deeds with the

---

[15] Eminent domain defined – *Black's Law Dictionary* – "The inherent power of a governmental entity to take privately owned property, esp. land, and convert it to public use, subject to reasonable compensation for the taking."

Public Land Records Division you have literally turned your private property into public land. Do you see the difference?

In England, no one outside of the King or the royal family holds property in Allodial title, because the crown owns all of the land. In the United States; however, most land is not held in Allodial title, as evidenced by the existence of property taxes. In France, while Allodial title existed before the French Revolution, it was rare and limited to ecclesiastical properties like that of churches and property that had fallen out of feudal ownership. Did you catch that last part? Even if you did, it is worth repeating, "…property that had fallen out of feudal ownership". Remember, currently in the United States we hold property in Fee Simple, as part of the feudal system. Interestingly enough, Quebec adopted a form of Allodial title when it abolished feudalism in the mid-nineteenth century. Allodial title is used to distinguish between the absolute ownership of land by individuals from that of feudal ownership where property ownership is dependent on a relationship to a lord or superior. Wait a second! Didn't the founding fathers already fight to free us from this type of serfdom and/or slavery? Webster's first dictionary states that allodium is, "land which is absolute property of the owner, real estate held in absolute independence, without being subject to any rent, service, or acknowledgement to a superior. It is thus opposed to the feudal system of ownership." Property owned under Allodial title today, by way of a Land Patent[16], is referred to as Allodial land or Allodium. Therefore, this process needs to be corrected in order for the American people to once again regain there rights, liberties, and freedom.

---

[16] Land Patent – is a document issued by government that passes as evidence of title to individual parcels of public land. Some patentees bought their land for cash, others homesteaded a claim, and still others came into ownership via one of the many donation acts that Congress passed to transfer public lands to private ownership.

IN PLAIN SIGHT THE DISREGARDED TRUTH

It saddens me that the majority of the American people are so complacent and uninterested in understanding the truth when it concerns their rights. For some reason, they don't care to know how they are currently holding their property. Again, I wonder why? Apparently, the majority of people have been trained not to question anything, especially the documents that they are about to sign and agree to. It is imperative that the American people understand the differences between the titles that are being used today. It is also important that the American people fully understand that each owner, legal or equitable, has certain legal rights. For example, the person or persons occupying the property, even if that person is a renter, has been conveyed some of the equitable owners' rights. Do you recall the "bundle of rights" that I referred to earlier? These rights include the right of possession, right of control, right of enjoyment, etc. If you are an owner of a home and you decide to rent your house to another party, you would have effectively relinquished some of the "bundle of rights" that you possess as the equitable owner. You, however, do retain some of the rights as the equitable owner; like that of the right of disposition. This is your right to sell your interest in said property.

Some Lawyers and Real Estate Brokers continually disagree with these facts by stating that no property ownership works in this manner. However, they change their tune when this next situation is brought up and discussed. Therefore, to assure that this information is correct, all I have to do is point out that when a Land Trust is formed you know, that's if you are one of these professionals, that a Trustee is assigned to the trust. When this occurs the Trustee is the legal owner of the property within the trust, along with the trust itself. The person that had formed the trust is the beneficiary, which makes them the equitable owner of the trust. Furthermore, the law prohibits a party of a trust from being both, the legal and equitable owners. This situation immediately proves to these professionals that I am speaking the truth. Still, most people do not know that a Trustee has been assigned to their property, even though in most cases they are paying the property tax to such a person. Moreover, an additional Trustee is assigned when a financial institution or County Tax Assessor's Office moves forward to foreclose on your home? Anyone who is aware of the foreclosure process knows that a Trustee is assigned to your property when the foreclosure process begins. Therefore, if a Trustee has been assigned, when was your property placed into a trust? Furthermore, if you are indeed the legal owner, how did the government gain the authority to do such a thing? Could it be that you are not the legal owner and the government within your area is? Could it also be that the Deed of Trust that you filed with the Land Records Division has granted such authority? The answers to the last two questions are yes.

Another important fact that should be brought into consideration, concerning how unjust our system has become, is that there are people who have successfully paid off their mortgages and are now living on a fixed income. If property taxes continue to rise, along with the cost of living, they may find themselves losing their home. You may also find yourself, when the time comes for you to retire, not being able to keep your home after you have worked so hard to pay it off. This is completely unacceptable, especially when you had already paid a sales tax on the property when you bought it, along with other numerous fees. This was never the intent of property taxes nor was it the intent of a free America. Despite that, what do you actually receive from the State, County, or City governments for all the money that you have paid and are going to continue to pay? Do you receive anything that is actually tangible? Have you ever asked yourself this question? If you receive anything at all, you would continue to believe that what you do receive would justify you jeopardizing the ownership of your property? I, on the other hand, believe that you will support a change. Most people believe that they are getting public schools, a police force, and maybe a fire department. Property taxes were put in place to pay for the Sheriff's Department, not the municipal police departments, which we are all aware of today. In addition, most fire departments are voluntary non-profit organizations and, if they are not, they need to be. As for the public schools, they all need to be competing for your business; therefore, they should be privately owned and operated. If you disagree, I then urge you to see John Stossel's documentary on "Keeping America Stupid" before you make any judgments.

Mostly, unless you are living way out from the cities, the local governments continue to unjustly harassed people within their jurisdiction. The sad part is that the people that are being subjected to this type of harassment are the same people that are paying these government employee's salaries. Therefore, the government has created the following departments and agencies in order to oversee their property, which has had an unintended consequence of harassment upon the American people. These departments and agencies consist of, but are not limited to, the following:

- Zoning Boards
- Permit and Inspection Agencies
- Property Assessments and Taxing Agencies
- Health Departments
- Law Enforcement Agencies - Due to the issuance of no knock warrants; law enforcement officers can now enter your home without any warning whatsoever.

Maybe, at this point, you are starting to see that we need to make a change from this German Gestapo like tactic and acknowledge that we have lost site of the fact that property rights are the essence of both liberty and freedom. Some would say that the law requires us to record our deeds on public land records; however, that is not true. The Law is specifically clear on this issue. Doesn't the Constitution of the United States prohibit the States from interfering in our right to contract with one another, as stated earlier in a previous chapter? Yes, it does. Furthermore, there is no law that requires you to record the ownership of your property on public land records. So, with that said, why is it that most people do it? The answer has already been revealed, it is the requirement of the financial institution in which you had borrowed the money to purchase said property. Common sense will tell you that there's no law requiring such action, it's a contractual requirement that you had voluntarily entered into. This explains why so many people record their deeds and contracts on public land records. How many people do you know that can buy a house with cash? This is the purpose of keeping you poor. For if the governments of our country and the bankers themselves were to allow you to retain your wealth they would lose their control over the American people. Therefore, you and everyone else will become independent and free from debt, banking, and that of government, which they will not allow to happen. Taking legal ownership of your property, which is not limited to your home, allows them to control you and your family.

How's this for a solution? Lets get rid of all property taxes, outside of commercially held property, and allow the American people to own the property that they have worked so hard to acquire. In addition, let's require that the governments, both locally and federally, get their income from a legal Constitutional tax; like the sales tax? This will ensure that we will be able to secure our wealth, especially our homes. To implement this solution we must become united within our communities and elect a County Sheriff that will support this effort and actually defend and protect his or hers constituents. It really is that simple. We, as Americans, cannot correct the situation if we just keep ignoring and legitimizing the problem. We, once again, need to become the absolute owners of our property. Only then will we regain our rights, liberties, and freedom. I urge you to embrace the thought that taxing our homes is not the correct answer. This is, however, the most important piece of property you'll ever own. At least with sales taxes we can control how much of our wealth is spent.

"Private ownership of property is vital to both our freedom and our prosperity." *By Congresswoman Cathy McMorris Rodgers of the U.S. House of Representatives.*

Work Harder

So You Can Do Better For Yourself

Today, the above saying, which is used in casual conversations from time to time, does not apply to the average person working a 9 to 5 job, especially if you are paid on an hourly or salary basis. This is true for two very important reasons. The first reason is that, if you were to work overtime, more income taxes will be withheld from your paycheck than if you had not worked the overtime. The second reason is that, if you were to acquire a second job, you will pay more in income taxes than if you did not obtain the second position. So you tell me, does this saying apply to the average American employee? No, it does not! It cannot apply if you are penalized or punished for earning more money. Furthermore, if you are self-employed you may be under some illusion that this penalty does not apply to you. However, contrary to popular belief, a self-employed person, like that of an independent contractor or business person, may have a little more control of their money, but this penalty still applies to them and their business. If we, as a country, had remained on the gold and silver standard, which would have resulted in never giving the Federal Reserve Banks the ability to inflate our currency, a wage earner would indeed benefit from working harder. If you are currently a wage earner or if you have ever been employed you know that I am speaking the truth. The truth of the matter is that this problem would not exist if it were not for the Federal government creating an astronomical amount of debt, an income tax, and inflation[17]. For the most part, all of the above came into existence, during the year of 1913, when our Congress created the Federal Reserve Act, the Internal Revenue Act, and supposedly had passed the 16th Amendment to the U.S. Constitution. The problem started with the people within the Federal government and the deceptions portrayed by the owners of the Federal Reserve Banks. With that said, I would like to address the government's debt and the interest that they are paying; however, I want to save that issue for a later chapter titled "The Truth About Inflation and Banking".

It appears that the Bankers, with the help of the Federal government, have stacked the deck against the average American. To prove this, I'll give you an example. Over the years, as you work harder and harder to make a living, there may come a time where a government taxing agency makes a claim that you owe them back taxes, plus interest. Hopefully this never happens; however, there's an interesting fact about the interest on income taxes. This is where the deck is stacked against the American people. Why is it that the State and Federal taxing agencies are not required to pay you interest on the money that you had paid to them throughout the year, especially when they owe you a refund? I ask this because the tax that you had paid wasn't actually due until April 15th the following year. Would you ever put your money into a savings account with a bank and not expect interest on your money? Still,

---

[17] Inflation Defined - "An increase in the amount of currency in circulation, resulting in a relatively sharp and sudden fall in its value and rise in prices: it may be caused by an increase in the volume of paper money issued or of gold mined, or a relative increase in expenditures as when the supply of goods fails to meet the demand." *Webster's New Universal Unabridged Dictionary*.

the situation is completely different when you owe the IRS or the State. If you ever find yourself owing a tax, you'll have to pay the amount they claim that you owe, plus any penalties and INTEREST. Interest and penalties are nothing more than a tax on top of a tax. I thought we were entitled to a system of equal justice, not a system of corruption and extortion. It feels like the governments of our country have instructed the Judges to use a double-sided coin in making their decisions when dealing with the American people. It is organized crime at it's best.

In order to demonstrate how ridiculous the interest and penalties have become, I would like to tell you a story of what happened to a good friend of mine name Alex. My friend Alex and I were working together for the same employer and one day he received a tax bill from the State. I know this may sound silly at first, but it is true nonetheless. The tax bill was for $14.00 because, as according to the State taxing agency, Alex owed the State $7.00 more than allowed at the end of the year. Alex's total tax bill, which he paid in full, was $257.00. Wait, it gets better. Alex was so upset about this tax bill he decided to call the Comptroller's office. Alex and I setup a conference call, so that I could be part of the conversation. When Alex finally got in contact with a representative he asked, "Why did I get this bill?" The representative stated, "The reason why you received the tax assessment is because you owed us $257.00 upon the filing of your tax return and you were $7.00 over the limit. As for the $14.00, that's the interest and penalties for owing us $7.00". Apparently, there's a $250.00 limit that you are not allowed to go over, that's if you owe the State. Still, this is all due to and I quote, "We should have received the $7 during the year and not when you filed your tax return." I couldn't believe my ears. That's an overall 200% penalty! It is absurd to think that these taxing agencies can conduct illegal practices, which are extracting wealth from the American people by charging them an extortion fee. An important point to recognize is that, as an employee, no one knows what their tax liability is going to be. That is, until they

IN PLAIN SIGHT THE DISREGARDED TRUTH

complete the tax document, which is not to be completed until later the next year. What is even more confusing is that Alex was having the maximum amount withheld from his pay, but yet he was still being punished. This brings us to the most interesting part of this story. Alex asked the representative at the Comptroller's office, "Why am I being penalized because my employer failed to withhold the correct amount?" You will not believe the answer that the representative gave him. The representative stated, "Your employer is not authorized to be your withholding agent and you are responsible for your withholdings". Just for informational purposes, Alex was claiming zero and was having the maximum amount withheld from his pay. If what the representative said is true, then why are employers allowed to withhold a tax from their employees before the tax is actually due? More importantly, why would anyone allow an employer to withhold taxes from their pay when the employer is not authorized to do so?

Due to the above conversation, I researched the withholding laws and their regulations and found something very interesting. The representative, at the Comptroller's office, was correct about the penalties, interests, and the withholding requirements. There are penalties and interests for owing more than $250.00 at the end of the year, but there is NO law making anyone, outside of a corporation and non-resident alien, liable for such a tax. Furthermore, there is no law requiring any American to have money withheld from their paycheck pursuant to income taxes. So, the question still remains. Why would anyone allow their employer to withhold money from their paycheck when no law exists? Could it be the government has tricked the American people into focusing on the penalties and interests and not the actual liability to scare them into paying? Could the government's tactic of using fear have distracted the American people from questioning the liability to begin with? If so, this would be another deceitful act by the government. Even if a person was liable for such a tax, I thought the tax wasn't due until April 15th of the following year. If the tax isn't due until April 15th the following year, why is it that the American people are being penalized for being late with their payment? Could it be that we are being lied to about our tax system and how it is to operate? Are you required to pay your property tax before it is due? No, you are not. If you pay your property tax late are you penalized and charged interest? No, you are not. Only in certain cases where someone else has paid your tax liability are you required to pay interest. Furthermore, are you penalized for not paying your property tax throughout the year? Again, no you are not. In spite of everything, why is it that the county governments allow you to keep your money throughout the year, when it concerns property taxes, but the Federal and State taxing agencies require you to pay the income tax in advance of the actual due date? I'll tell you why. The taxing agencies of both the local and Federal governments know, when it pertains to the income tax, that they are taxing you heavily and, more importantly, illegally. They know that if they did not trick the employer into withholding pursuant to the Social Security Tax Act that you and ever other American would feel the burden and pain of paying this incredible amount. They do not want you to wake up and feel the fire. They want you to bleed to death financially, all without you understanding what's going on. This is the primary way, outside of inflation, that allows them to control your amount of wealth.

Even though it is true, as addressed in a previous chapter, that the State and County governments own the legal aspect of our property, this next example, which was taken from a local newspaper, proves that our government could not care less about protecting us. If anything, it proves how they, meaning the government, can legally rob, steal, and extort money from the American people, all without any consequences to their actions. In order to prove how ridiculous our system has become, read the following article literally and, more importantly, with a sense of morality.

In Plain Sight The Disregarded Truth

City Takes, Then Sells Woman's Truck

Feb 23, 2007

BALTIMORE, MD - *Three unpaid parking tickets cost a woman her Ford truck. When this Woman, of Columbia, went to retrieve her 1999 Ford F-250, the city had auctioned it off. A vehicle, with an estimated Kelly Blue Book value of $6,700, sold for $2,500. Somebody got a great steal. And it sure wasn't the "Owner". "I'm still in shock," she told Reporters. "I can't believe I lost my truck for a couple of parking tickets." The "Owner" parked her truck in front of a friend's house in West Baltimore on Sept. 26, 2006. Four hours later, she said, it vanished. Believing the F-250 was stolen, the "Owner", called Baltimore Police Department. After filling out a report and checking the impound lots, police promised to call if the vehicle turned up. After a month of checking with the city, the "Owner" finally received a call, but not from the police. "Someone called on my cell phone and asked me if I wanted to buy my truck back for $3,000," she said. It gets worse. The Owner found out that, despite the stolen-vehicle report, the city had towed her truck to its impound lot on Pulaski Highway for three unpaid parking tickets that totaled $574 in fines. That's the city's policy. Three tickets, and your vehicle is towed. When the "Owner" complained, city officials cited a certified letter receipt signed by her. They say the "Owner" knew the car was there. The "Owner" says she never signed anything. "I told them it wasn't my signature, I never received the letter," she said. The United States Postal Service agreed. Adrienne Barnes, spokeswoman for the Department of Transportation, said the city was simply following procedures. "City law gives us authorization to dispose of a vehicle within 45 days," she said. "We take steps to notify the owner. After the allotted time, the vehicle becomes a safety hazard." City Councilman Jack Young, District 12, doesn't see it that way.*

And he's looking forward to a showdown with DOT officials March 1 at a hearing on his resolution that calls for city officials to explain why cars are sold so quickly. "We can't just sell people's cars because we can't get in touch with them," he said. "It's a lame excuse. We should use whatever means necessary to contact people." End of Article

Before we get into the purpose of why I added this article, I have to ask a few questions concerning this incident.

1. First of all, if the "Owner" actually owned the vehicle and the vehicle was taken from her, isn't this grand theft auto?

2. The City seized a vehicle that was worth $6,700.00 and then they sold it for $2,500.00, all because the so-called "Owner" allegedly owed the City $574.00. That's a profit in the amount of $1,926.00 for the city. Therefore, did the "Owner" receive the $1,926.00?

3. Does it make it legal or morally correct because the City was following procedures?

4. Councilman Jack Young wants the City to explain why vehicles are being sold so quickly. You have to be kidding me! The question should be; why are they stealing and selling other people's property to begin with? Isn't this to be considered theft?

The reason why I brought up the vehicle issue is to show that, even though you have worked hard to acquire your property, the governments of our country can take your property at any time, without consequences for their actions. Even though this is true, why is it okay that a government entity can take someone's vehicle, without a court order? If the Owner of the Ford F-250 had owed the City for any other debt there would have been a collections hearing or even a court hearing. If a person (the debtor) has an outstanding debt to another party (the creditor), the creditor will always need to file a lawsuit in order to retrieve money, which may result in a lien being placed on the debtor's property. What this means is that the debtor will not be able to sell his or her property without first paying off the outstanding debt to the creditor. The governments of our country need to follow the laws that apply to everyone else. The point that I am trying to convey is that it is not okay for any government to take anyone's property without first using the lawful legal system. This means that no one will have to worry about their property being taken without their knowledge, at least from government thugs. It appears the governments of our country have purposely circumvented the legal system, by way of tricking the American people into relinquishing their legal rights to property. As a result, this has allowed the governments the ability to engage themselves in a criminal activity. It's not okay for us, the American people, to take someone's property without first going to court. So, why is it okay for the government? Still, in the situation of the Ford F-250, the person involved no longer has transportation and may be inhibited in getting to work. Oh yeah, I forgot. The government couldn't care less. This proves that today's governments are no longer acting in the best interest of the American people. Furthermore, they are no longer interested in protecting the people that they had once sworn to protect.

Over the years I have spoken with thousands of people about the issue of direct taxes and how they have been placed upon our property. Although some people will not agree that direct taxes are an illegal theft of someone's property they will, however, agree that direct taxes are a LEGAL theft of someone's property. How absurd is that? Legal or otherwise, it's still THEFT. The American people need to stop justifying an illegal act by calling it legal! All direct taxes are morally and ethically wrong, period! Still, with all of the taxes that we pay, you'll be surprised to find out that you are also paying a secret tax. Yes a secret tax. The secret tax will be revealed in the chapter titled "The Truth About Inflation and Banking".

In summary, if a government entity can take your property, especially without a court order and without going through the County Sheriff, then you cannot be the legal or absolute owner. If, however, you are still having a difficult time believing that the governments of our country would create and maintain such an illusionary tactic, all you need to do is open your eyes, look at the facts, and stop listening to all the propaganda. Remember, if it walks like a duck and looks like… ahh, you know what I mean. The solution is to become a true tea partier, unlike the people that claim to be today, and start pouring out your tea. If the Federal government has the ability to print money as it sees fit then why do they need to tax your income? The answer has already been revealed. They don't. It is a scheme to keep you poor and under control.

Here's a solution. Why don't we allow everyone the ability to keep what they have earned, so that they will have more wealth and an easier life? The majority of the American people will then be able to appreciate the assets that they have acquired, as opposed to dreading the liabilities of today. This will in turn create more wealth throughout America, which will allow the people the ability to give to the disadvantaged. If, on the other hand, you know someone who believes that it is a bad idea to allow the American people to become self-sufficient would prove that such a person to be a socialist, which has either been brainwashed, who is seeking power, or is inherently lazy. Therefore, you need to stay away from such a person, so that we may restore our country back to its original intent.

Democracy or Republic
You'll Be Surprised!

This chapter will challenge most of the American people's beliefs, as to the structure of our country and the foundation that created The United States of America. Therefore, I must reveal that this will be an eye-opening topic, that's if you don't already know the truth. Furthermore, I am once again calling upon your logical reasoning, so that the truth may be revealed. I am also calling upon your courage of wanting to know the truth. Still, why am I preparing you for this chapter? I am doing so, because I know how it feels to have your underlying beliefs challenged with a preponderance of evidence that proves your beliefs to be incorrect. For that reason, I hope that you will have an open mind when reading the interesting facts concerning this issue. Even though some of the information contained in this chapter may appear to be negative in nature; you are about to be informed of one of the most positive aspects of our country. Nevertheless, I have to congratulate the news media, public schools, and the government for doing an outstanding job in confusing the American people into believing that the United States of America is a Democracy. How often have you heard government officials come on television and refer to our country as a Democracy? If you watch the news, you've probably heard it on a daily basis. The problem is that most of the American people believe that the United States of America is indeed a Democracy, which couldn't be further from the truth. I wonder why the governments of our country, the news media networks, and public schools tend to mislead the American people into believing such a thing. Could there be a reason as to why they would mislead the American people?

Still, for those of you that may find it difficult to believe that our country is not a Democracy, the simplest way to prove this argument is to ask you if you know the Pledge of Allegiance. With that said, do you know it? Even though I have asked this question, I am in no way advocating any pledge. Just in case you don't know it word for word, let's start out by saying it together. "I pledge allegiance to the flag of the United States of America and to the Republic for which it stands..." STOP!!! Did you or did you not just say, "to the Republic for which it stands"? The Pledge does NOT read and to the "Democracy" for which it stands; therefore, why do most of the American people believe that our country, as a whole, is a Democracy? For most of us, we've been saying the pledge for a good portion of our lives and we still haven't been able to put two and two together. Wouldn't you have to agree that it's sad that most of us, the American people, are so ignorant and lack the intelligence to comprehend something so simple as to see the truth for what it really is? I, on the other hand, don't believe that to be the case. I believe that the majority of people have the intelligence to comprehend the truth. However, if my belief is correct, could it be that the brainwashing from the news media and the government itself is so unrelenting that most of us are having problems with seeing through the lies? That very well could be a possibility. When was the last time, if you can remember, you heard someone refer to our country as a Republic? It is happening more today than ever before, but when speaking of years past I can only recall a few times.

When I was young, an early teenager at most, I used to hear people talk about our Republic. The result of being so young was that I was not interested in listening to their conversations. Needless to say, years later, I noticed that I was no longer hearing anyone talking about our Republic. I used to say to myself, I wonder why. Do you recall the old saying; "ignorance is bliss"? Well, I am here to tell you that ignorance is not bliss; it just leads to frustration.

Years ago, the difference between a Republic and a Democracy was once widely understood, especially with Americans. It was so important that everyone knew the differences that the Federal government actually printed a manual on the subject. The U.S. War Department, now known today as The Department of Defense, taught the differences between the two in a training manual No. 2000-25, published on November 30, 1928. Not only did the Federal government define Democracy; they even went on to explain why democracies fail. Still, the following information has come from the same government that now advocates that we have the greatest Democracy ever. With that said, you might be asking yourself, what is the difference? Well, let's take a look at how the Federal government defined a Democracy in their Training manual. Washington D.C., November 30, 1928. M2000-25, 118-120 Citizenship:

> *"Democracy: a government of the masses, authority derived through mass meeting or any other form of direct expression, results in mobocracy, attitude towards property is communistic-negating property rights, attitude toward all is that the will of the majority shall regulate..."*

> *"Why Democracies Fail - A Democracy cannot exist as a permanent form of government. It can only exist until the voters discover they can vote themselves largess [money, gifts, and earmarks] out of the public treasury. From that moment on, the majority always votes for the*

candidates promising the most benefits from the public treasury with the result that Democracy always collapses over a loose physical policy, always to be followed by a dictatorship." [More correctly an Oligarchy, not a dictatorship] Oligarchy is defined on the next page in the footnote.

For your viewing, a copy of the document has been added below:

CITIZENSHIP   **TM 2000–25**
                                               115–120

Democracy:
A government of the masses.
Authority derived through mass meeting or any other form of "direct" expression.
Results, in mobocracy.
Attitude toward property is communistic — negating property rights.
Attitude toward law is that the will of the majority shall regulate, whether it be based upon deliberation or governed by passion, prejudice, and impulse, without restraint or regard to consequences.
Results in demagogism, license, agitation, discontent, anarchy.

Democracy is the "direct" rule of the people and has been repeatedly tried without success.

This is a definition that you will not learn in a public school. Therefore, a Democracy is the rule of the majority and the people's attitude toward property ownership is communistic, it attempts to negate all rights thereof. The attitude toward the law, in a Democracy, is that the majority shall regulate with no consideration to the consequences of violating other peoples' rights, liberties, and freedoms. A Democracy is a temporary form of government and has been tried repeatedly without success. The reason for its failures is that a Democracy is not a form of government, as some would believe. Democracy, in itself, is a means of operations. It is the process on how decisions are made, voting for example. To say that we have a democratic form of government is not an incorrect statement, because the people within our government use the means of voting to resolve any conflict between the parties. Remember, the majority rules.

In a free society, the democratic process can only exist within a governmental entity or within a voluntarily created organization, like that of a Home Owners Association or a private club. If a Democracy is used as the structure of government it will only be used as the transition from a free country to an enslaved society ruled by a few, which in itself is an Oligarchy.[18]   When the democratic process is wrongfully used as a form of government it will collapse, because it cannot maintain itself for a long period of time. Why? This is due to the people, both within government and the private sector, becoming aware that they can easily gain access to public funds and; therefore, they will spend it freely, without any consequences to their actions. Furthermore, once they start to run out of money they will use force against the remaining population to gain additional funds, again without any consequences to their actions. All the same, doesn't this sound familiar? If so, there's a reason why.

The reason for the similarity of what I just explained and what is happening today is that the governments of our country are acting outside of their authority, by imposing a democratic form of government upon the American people. The Law, the Constitution of the United States of America, forbids this type of interaction. The Constitution forbids the governments of our country from interacting with the people in the private sector in any other way than a Republican form of interaction. The Democratic form of interaction means the majority of people will rule the minority. This type of interaction has been made illegal, at least within the 50

---

[18] Oligarchy – "a form of government in which the ruling power belongs to a few persons." Webster's Dictionary, third College Edition. Oligarchy – "A government in which a small group of persons exercises control…" Black's Law Dictionary, Seventh Edition.

States. The founders believed that a law prohibiting the democratic form of interaction between a government entity and a free person was required. Therefore, such a law was created, passed, and still exists today. Yet, most of the American people do not know of its existence. On the other hand, some people know of its existence, but they have no clue as to what it means. This law limits the authority of the government, both locally and federally, so that the majority of people will not have the authority to decide your fate. The reasons for these limitations are threefold. This Law was passed to ensure the private sector would retain their sovereignty and control over the government, that equal rights would be preserved, and that the majority rule would never again be able to raise its ugly head. As we notice the similarities of why a Democracy fails and as to what is happening to our country today, could there be a reason? Could the reason for the similarities be that our system of laws, equal justice, and our Constitutional Republic have been eroded to the point of non-existence? Could it be that our Constitutional Republic has now truly turned into a Democracy, allowing its ugly head to rise once again? Are we also witnessing, during this transition, the collapse of our once free America? Are the similarities also telling us that a shift in power from the American people to a few people, called the elite, is occurring? I believe that it is. There are only two reasons why such a betrayal to ones country would occur. The first is the people that have found themselves within "our" government have become corrupt, due to greediness and their quest for power. The second is that the people, as a whole, are too weak to stop it. The important part to understand is that all of the injustices that are occurring are taking place under a Democracy [19] and not under our Constitutional Republic.

---

[19] Democracy – "Rule by the majority". *Webster's Dictionary. U.S. Government Training manual war Department, No 2000-25. Washington, November 30, 1928. M2000-25, 118-120 Citizenship*

Even if the 50 States of the Union were indeed a Democracy, you wouldn't like it anyway. That is with the understanding that you are now starting to recognize the truth as to what makes up a Democracy and assuming that you are not a socialist[20]. With that said, I should explain. The most important aspect of a Democracy is that its structure is based off of the majority rules mentality, whether right or wrong. There's no difference between a Democracy and that of two wolves and a sheep standing around debating as to what's for dinner. That may be funny to some, but it's not funny to me when it concerns my rights, liberties and freedom. How about you? Does this type of mentality bother you at all? How does it make you feel that currently, due to the socialistic mentality, the majority of other human beings can take your rights, liberties, and freedom away, at any point in time? If 51% of the American people agree to take the other 49% of the American people's property and give it to the poor or to a wealthy corporation it will be completely legal. In a Democracy, if 51% of the people were to agreed to make all firearms illegal, the ownership of firearms will be illegal, no matter if you disagree or not. Furthermore, they will use force and take the firearms from the remaining 49% that do not agree with their intent. Yet again, this is all "legal" under a Democracy. Can you believe that this type of behavior can go without punishment?

Even though, the majority of people would have broken the law, with the implementation of their illegal act, there is only one reason why their act would remain legal. The people within the private sector would have done nothing to correct the injustice. If an illegal act goes without correction that illegal act apparently becomes legal, due to the fact that there was no one accountable for

---

[20] Socialist - a person who believes in Socialism, all of which is a system in which essential industries, social services, property and the distribution of wealth are publicly and cooperatively owned and democratically controlled and not individually. No matter how hard you work you'll never get ahead. Socialism has been identified with communist. *Wikipedia - the free encyclopedia.*

breaking the law nor was anyone punished for such an act. Yet again, it's quite simple. The actions taken by government today conflict with the Supreme Law of them all and; therefore, their acts are illegal. The only reason why they are getting away with their crimes on humanity is due to the American people's ignorance and fear. Are we starting to see the beginnings of a new Gestapo or Mafia, where innocent people are being victimized? It appears that our country has turned from a righteous and free one to an unethical and immoral nation, all because of a democratic and socialistic mindset. The majority rule is always described as a feature of a Democracy, but without responsible individuals within government it is entirely possible for the rights of the minority to be abused by the tyranny of the majority. Once the transition has taken place, from a Democracy to an Oligarchy[21], the minority will trample upon the inherent rights and liberties of the American people.

It confuses me as to why any American would not see this as an important issue. I say that it is important because without liberty and freedom to prosper we will end up like Rome. Could it be that most people don't care because they don't understand the difference between a Democracy and a Constitutional Republic? If so, this is the reason for this book. Unlike in a Democracy, a Constitutional Republic has rules, that must be followed, and safe guards built into the creating document, which is called The Constitution. That means that neither the minority nor the majority of the American people can take away your rights, your property, or your liberties without due process[22] of law. In addition, our Constitutional

[21] Oligarchy – "a form of government in which the ruling power belongs to a few persons." Webster's Dictionary, third College Edition. Oligarchy – "A government in which a small group of persons exercises control..." *Black's Law Dictionary, Seventh Edition.*

[22] Due Process – "The conduct of legal proceedings according to established rules and principles for the protection and enforcement of private rights, including notice and the right to a fair hearing." *Black's Law dictionary seventh edition.*

Republic is based on basic principles of truth, equal justice, and common sense. Another way to explain the difference between a Democracy and a Republic is to whom is sovereign over the other. In a Republic, the people hold sovereign power individually which means each individual person is "endowed by his creator with unalienable rights". These rights can never be taken away by a majority vote. The sole purpose of a republican form of government is to secure those individual rights. In a Democracy, sovereign power is invested collectively in the group as a whole. Therefore, in a Democracy you will always have a dictator, even though the dictator is in the form of the majority of people. Unlike in an Oligarchy were the dictator is the minority. A good example of this is in a homeowners association. If you have ever lived in a homeowners association you know what I am talking about. In the case of a structured Democracy, like that of a homeowners association, the dictator is in the form of the small minority, the board members. Why do I say this? Well, if you're a realist then you would know and understand that the people in these positions couldn't care less if you vote on a project or not. They are going to do what they feel is in the best interest of the community, no matter if it is wrong or not.

As you can see, Democracy in itself is a means of operation, which is the process in which decisions are made. To be more specific, it is the process of voting. The sad part is when this type of mentality has started to surface outside of government, the government itself will unjustly enter into the lives of the law-abiding people by using, what I call, the rule of emotion rather than using logic, reason, and that of the law itself. These socialists will then trample upon the inherent rights and liberties of the so-called free people. Again, does this sound familiar? Isn't this what's happening today? The founders knew that if the process of Democracy were to ever come outside of the internal workings of the government that no one person, in the private sector, would be safe and/or protected by the abuses of government. Therefore, the Law prohibiting such behavior was created.

Another important fact of a Democracy is that the rules and laws change constantly. It's exactly what some of the judges say in their courtrooms today, "The law is what I say the law is" or "I will instruct the jury as to what the law is." If you've never heard these sayings for yourself that means you haven't spent any time in a courtroom. The laws in a true Democracy are politically created, which for the most part are driven by emotion, and reflect absolutely no truth or justice. They only reflect power and nonsensical ideas. Take gun control and drug laws as prime examples. They are solely based on an emotional reaction to a perceived problem for which the misuse of guns and drugs are merely a symptom. Despite the overwhelming facts and evidence that these laws do not work, but actually encourage disobedience to such laws, those who support these unjust laws demand more laws in the face of their repeated failures. For example, do you think that gun laws actually stop criminals from obtaining illegal guns? No, they do not. Out of all the laws that are currently on the books today, I suggest that we revisit the gun and drug laws. These laws are a perfect example of an emotional mindset, which promotes nonsensical ideas that borders insanity. I am in no way excluding any other law that is also unjust and/or insane. I am just merely pointing out the most immoral, unjust, and abused set of laws that exist today. Do you really think that drug laws actually stop people from using and selling drugs? Again, no they do not. The consequence of implementing such laws, that most people fail to see, is that these laws are causing a higher number of people that are being placed within our jails and prisons. These institutions are being filled up with people who merely wanted to use a drug for whatever reason, which is only harmful to the user of such drug. This consequence is directly reflective of the democratic process that has now entered the private sector. To deny such truths would be a prime example of someone's insanity. Therefore, due to these unjust laws, the governments of our country are extorting money and property from the remaining so-called free people in order to fund their immoral, dishonorable, and unethical operations, all with threats of violence and the use of force. This is a prime example of what will happen when the process of Democracy is allowed to enter into the private sector, which has been accomplished today.

In a Democracy people vote for what they want not for what is right. Believe it or not, there's a difference between right and wrong, even in the political realm. In addition, Democracy always blurs the principles of what is believed by the people in the private sector with that of the unjust principles of the people within government, in order to make them appear to be the same. This is a deceptive tactic that a Democracy has to use in order to justify itself. For example, take gambling laws. Is it okay for a State to involve itself in gambling practices, but it's not okay for anyone else? It's the old saying, "do as I say, don't do as I do" mentality. Individual rights and liberties, if they exist at all today, are relatively weak and have now taken the form of privileges granted through governmental licensing and the issuing of permits. Keep in mind that these privileges, which have been granted to you, can be taken away at any point in time. Therefore, remember this. What's legal today may not be legal tomorrow and an individual considered a law-abiding citizen one day may find himself or herself a criminal the next. That's a Democracy in a nutshell.

Do you still think a Democracy is a good thing? More importantly, are you going to continue with the belief that our country's system of governmental interaction was implemented as a democracy? Furthermore, do you believe that the intent of The United States of America was to be a socialistic system of lies, where you don't have the ability to own property or do what you want so long as you don't hurt another? No! I'm glad to hear that. If, on the other hand, you know someone that would disagree, than they are nothing more than a socialist pig. With that said, let me define what a socialist pig is. A socialist pig is a person who wants to have rights, liberties, and freedom, but at the same time wants the government to forcefully take money and/or wealth from other people and give it to them in the form of a socialist program, all in the name of safety and/or the general welfare. A person that meets these qualifications is basically a communist due to their support of an illegal, unjust, and immoral application of force used against innocent people. Furthermore, if you were to take a closer look at such an individual you will find that they are a nosey, controlling, and confused person. In a Constitutional Republic[23], even though small democracies exist within the governments, one supreme law rules the body of law as a whole. In the case of our country it's The Constitution of the United States of America, the supreme law of them all. That's why we do not live in just a Republic; we live in a Constitutional Republic. In essence, this law reflects equal justice and preserves the freedom of each and every individual human being, which for the most part is based on the Common Law. Therefore, if the government wanted to change the law they know that they would have to answer to a higher authority, the people, before doing so. This Law was discovered not created out of thin air, unlike our currency today. It's based on recognizing the difference between what is right and wrong. It was designed to be fair, honest, and, more importantly, to show the truth. The founders of our country knew that human nature would never change. The nature that I am referring to is the nature to control others. What was okay and legal yesterday should be so today and tomorrow. The Law controls the government within a Republic; therefore, the government cannot control the law itself.

---

[23] Republic defined – "A system of government in which the people hold sovereign power and elect representatives who exercise that power. It contrasts on the one hand with a pure democracy, in which the people or community as an organized whole wield the sovereign power of government, and on the other with the rule of one person such as a king." Black's Law dictionary, seventh edition

Even though a small group of people would say that our government is indeed a Republican form of government, I would have to disagree. Why is that? Well let's look at the facts. When Congress proposes a new law a vote has to take place. Well, in order for a law to be passed by the Senate they would need the majority vote. That's why I say there's a small Democracy within our Constitutional Republic. Therefore, for some reason, the governments, both federally and locally, would have you believe that the entire system is a Democracy. This is the deceptive tactic that I was referring to earlier, which brings up another important question. Why would the Federal government want the American people to believe that the entire system is a Democracy? I believe that I have the answer to this question. The Federal government believes that they can do whatever they want, so long as they accomplish two goals. The first is to keep you ignorant to the truth about our Constitutional Republic. The second is to make sure that you do not know what your rights, liberties, and freedom consist of. Yet again, this is another deceptive tactic being used by the Democracy. In our Constitutional Republic, The Constitution of the United States of America and that of State Constitutions restrict the governments of our country. Even though the people have given the governments the power to carry out their assigned functions within these documents they are, however, limited. There's a reason for the limitations that were placed upon the governments and that was to ensure that the ultimate moral authority would remain outside of the political structure, with the people. The government's primary role and purpose is to protect rights, liberties, and to defend the lives and property of every person living within our country. Rights and liberties cannot be repealed or restrained by human laws; that's because rights are derived from a greater power than that of government. Rights and liberties are never granted by government, they are only to be protected by government. All the same, do you recall the War Departments training manual and how it defined

Democracy? This same document has also defined what a Republic is.

In summary; Republic: governmental authority is derived by the people; the attitude toward individual and property rights are respected; the attitude toward law is with fixed principles and established evidence, with strict regard to consequences; A Republic avoids tyranny; but yet results in liberty, reason, equal justice and contentment; a Constitutional Republic is superior to all others.

Wow! That sounded pretty good, didn't it? I don't know about you, but that's what I want!

TM 2000-25
120-121   CITIZENSHIP

Republic:

Authority is derived through the election by the people of public officials best fitted to represent them.

Attitude toward property is respect for laws and individual rights, and a sensible economic procedure.

Attitude toward law is the administration of justice in accord with fixed principles and established evidence, with a strict regard to consequences.

A greater number of citizens and extent of territory may be brought within its compass.

Avoids the dangerous extreme of either tyranny or mobocracy.

Results in statesmanship, liberty, reason, justice, contentment, and progress.

Is the "standard form" of government throughout the world.

Our Constitutional fathers, familiar with the strength and weakness of both autocracy and democracy, with fixed principles definitely in mind, defined a representative republican form of government. They "made a very marked distinction between a republic and a democracy * * * and said repeatedly and emphatically that they had founded a republic."

As you can see, it also states that a, "Democracy is the "direct" rule of the majority of people and has been repeatedly tried without success." Keep in mind, that as a person that has worked in law enforcement, I can tell you that most of the government officials do not care about you, your property, or your rights. So, how can they respect you? For crying out loud, they don't even respect the Law. You can prove this for yourself; it's in plain sight. Just look around and you will see the truth. They don't even understand the law or the underlying principles of our country. If this is true, which it is, how can any government employee or official respect you and your property? It's simple; they can't. It's sad to see that most of the government employees and officials do not understand the basic principles of what makes up our free America. Sadly enough, this includes most of the Judges, Attorneys, and Sheriffs. Can you now see how the collective mentality of both the local and federal governments have destroyed the principles of law and have blurred the distinction between what is right and wrong? In a Constitutional Republic, the thought of a collective sovereignty cannot exist, for if it did the individual private rights would not be supreme nor would they exist. Also, in a Constitutional Republic, the government is an instrument solely for security purposes in which the people are to be served rather than regulated. This would also include being represented rather than being ruled. If the principles of our Republican form of government were being followed, like in years past when our country was the wealthiest country in the world, the free market would create more businesses, more jobs, and more manufacturing ventures. In return, we would once again be the wealthiest country in the world and, more importantly, the practice of liberty would be untouched. If a Republic did not have a body of law to govern the government it would be the exact same thing as a Democracy. As we can see, the only difference between a Democracy and a Constitutional Republic is that a Democracy does not protect or guarantee anything. It is truly the rule of the majority.

What we have learned is that in a Republic, specifically a Constitutional Republic, there are certain rights and liberties that have been identified and are specifically protected from government intervention or involvement. Let me rephrase. In a Constitutional Republic the rights of the people are protected, they are NOT granted by the Constitution nor does the government itself grant them. The founding fathers knew that the worst threat that we would ever face would be from our own government. For this reason, there are numerous checks and balances enumerated within the Constitution of the United States of America. They are the decentralization of their power, the free and open elections, and trial by jury, among others. This also includes the right of the Citizens to keep and bear arms. That's why we have the Second Amendment. None of these checks and balances will ever be successful unless one thing happens. The American people must be aware of their responsibility and duty to keep the government in check. If, for some reason, the people were to fail in protecting our Constitution a socialistic Democracy will most certainly over write our Constitutional Republic, which will ultimately lead to an Oligarchy. History has proven this time and time again! Ironically, this will all be implemented against the will of the majority of the American people.

Now that you know the truth and the differences between a Democracy and a Republic, I must again clarify a statement that I made earlier. This is where I make the claim that a small Democracy is contained within our Republic. The Democracy that I am referring to is identified as Washington D.C. or any other area that the Federal government has exclusive jurisdiction and authority over. If you are currently living within one of these territories you are actually living within a Democracy. The additional areas that the Federal government has exclusive jurisdiction over include Guam, American Samoa, the Commonwealth of Puerto Rico, the Virgin Islands, and any one of the military bases around the world. You're probably saying to yourself right now, "I don't live in any of those areas?" Well, neither do I. For if I was, I would be living in a federal enclave[24] or, should I say, an insular possession[25]. Basically,

---

[24] Federal enclave – "territory or land that a State has ceded to the United States. Examples of federal enclaves are military bases, national parks, federally administered highways, and federal Indian reservations. The U.S. government has exclusive authority and jurisdiction over federal enclaves." *Black's Law dictionary, seventh edition.*

that means an area of land that the Federal government owns outright or has been granted exclusive jurisdiction over. Therefore, if you are living within the borders of the United States of America, meaning within one of the 50 states, but outside of Washington D.C. and outside of any federal enclave or insular possession then you are living within a Republic, a Constitutional Republic. Some would say that, "I live in Washington D.C. and; therefore, I live within the United States." Oh, really? Washington D.C. is not a State, it was ceded to the Federal government and they have exclusive jurisdiction over that land; therefore, it is in itself a Democracy and not part of the 50 States. That's right, it's a Democracy. Even though it sometimes borders an Oligarchy. Now, now... calm down, I said sometimes.

In general, common sense tells us that all military bases belong to the Federal government. The Federal government has full jurisdiction over these military bases. Wherever there's a military base, within any one of the 50 States, the individual State had ceded that area to the Federal government for that purpose. If, for some reason, you are living within Washington D.C. you are probably paying taxes without representation. This is one of the biggest complaints that Washington D.C. residents have. For crying out loud, it's even written on their license plates.

---

25 Insular possession – "a territorial dominion of a state or nation." "An island territory of the United States, such as Puerto Rico." *Black's Law Dictionary, Seventh Edition*

As you can see above, the basic Washington D.C. license plate states, "Taxation Without Representation", at the bottom. This is the District of Columbia's motto. Just like North Carolina's is "First in Flight", New Hampshire's is "Live Free or Die", and Florida reads the "Sunshine State". Wow! Try saying that last one about Florida ten times real fast. Still, why do you think that the residents of Washington D.C. do not have any representation? Again, if the public schools were doing their job properly, I wouldn't have had to ask the question. The answer is quite simple, Washington D.C. is not a State of the Union. In essence, it's a Country within a Country. As a result, none of the residents of Washington D.C. have the right to representation as guaranteed by the Federal Constitution. Washington D.C. is a Democracy because the Federal government has the ability to vote on whatever issue they see fit to vote on. They can close any road within this area, that's if the majority of officials agree. However, it is a fact, unless martial law has been declared, that the Federal government cannot come outside of Washington D.C. and close a road in any one of the fifty States. This is unless the State has given permission to the Federal government to do so. The key to understanding this concept is that if the Federal government were to interact with anyone outside of this area, meaning outside of Washington D.C. or any military base, they are at that point required by law to interact with the American people in a Republican form of interaction. Article 4, section 4, of the Constitution of the United States specifically states, "the United States shall guarantee to every State in this Union a Republican form of Government". What does this mean? This means that the government and its representatives are required to follow the law as it is written. They cannot just take you away, seize your wealth, or violate your rights without first affording you due process of law, which must be fair and unbiased. If the government were to come after you and your family, wouldn't you want the protections of due process? You don't have to answer that question, because I know you would. With that said, why are all the government officials, news reporters, and schoolteachers telling our children and us that we are living in the greatest Democracy? Again, I have an answer for this question. When a government official or news reporter makes a reference to our Democracy they do not know that they are making a reference to the inner workings of government and not to the actual structure in which we live in. Even though the word "Democracy" may be familiar to most, it is a concept that is misunderstood and misused by almost everyone. The only reason why a democratic system is being used is for the mere fact that the chances of getting everyone to agree are slim to none. Even though this is true, the majority can never take your freedom, liberty, and rights away within a Constitutional Republic. Nevertheless, which one do you want to live in? I hope you would want to live in our Constitutional Republic. Still, do you remember the statement that I wrote referencing a small fact in history, where I stated that a Democracy is only a temporary step between a Constitutional Republic and that of an Oligarchy? Well, wake up. It is happening today. Seriously, it is!

The final part concerning a Democracy is that the time frame of its existence cannot allow it to exist as a permanent form of government. This only applies when the government continues to interact with the people, in the private sector, in a democratic form. It is always used as a transitional stage in order to take control. In order to prove these facts, what do you think will happen when this so-called Democracy runs out of money or can no longer pay its debt. You guessed it. A new form of government will emerge. The sad part is that the founders had warned us about this possibility; however, it seems that the majority of the American people couldn't care less. And, for those of you that still do not believe that we were not intended to be an overall Democracy just read some of the founding documents. For starters, do the Declaration of Independence and The Constitution of the United States of America even mention the word Democracy? No, they do not! In addition, without getting into a whole bunch of quotes from the founding fathers about how they felt about a Democracy, I'll just give you a synopsis. The founding fathers were extremely knowledgeable and experienced on the issues of a Democracy and they all feared a Democracy as much as a Monarchy.[26] They understood that the only entity that could take away the freedom the American people enjoy on a day-to-day basis would be by their own government. This would take place by either not being able to protect the people from foreign threats or by becoming too powerful and taking over every aspect of the American people's lives. Again, does this sound familiar? What do you think is happening today? Take a moment and look around. Listen carefully to the news and to the people around you. It will become clear to you soon. Still, I have a recommendation for you. Remember what I am saying to you now when you reach the chapter titled "War on Terrorism".

In final thoughts of this chapter, remember that The Declaration of Independence states in part, "We hold these truths to be self-evident, that all men are created equal, that they are endowed by their CREATOR with certain UNALIENABLE[27] Rights, that among these are Life, Liberty and the pursuit of Happiness ... That to secure these rights, Governments are instituted among Men, DERIVING THEIR JUST POWERS FROM THE CONSENT OF THE GOVERNED, ... That whenever any Form of Government becomes destructive of these ends, it is the Right of the People to alter or to abolish it, and to institute new Government..."

In all seriousness, now that you are aware of the differences between a Democracy and a Constitutional Republic which one would you want to have? If you ever stated in the past that you live

---

[26] Monarchy – "a government in which a single person rolls, with powers varying from absolute dictatorship to the merely ceremonial." *Black's Law dictionary, seventh edition.*

[27] Unalienable - see inalienable – "not transferable or assignable also termed unalienable". *Black's Law dictionary, seventh edition.*

in a Democracy will you continue to say that in the future? Lastly, now that the differences are clear, how can anyone defend a Democracy when you possess the ability to have a Republic? So again, which one do you want to live in? Still, I am stunned as to how many of my fellow Americans don't even know what their rights consist of, let alone the difference between a Democracy and a Constitutional Republic. Do you think I can blame them? Yes I can. For if they do not know what their rights are, how can they defend the rights of others? The sad part about all of this is that most people, due to the educational system, have no idea what liberty means. This is especially true when it concerns law enforcement officers, military personnel, and government employees and officials. If none of these people know what my rights consist of nor do they have any idea as to what liberty means, then how are they going to protect what is rightfully mine? That's the question that everyone should be asking his or her County Sheriff.

The Truth About Inflation and Banking

The information that is contained within this chapter will be, at the least, a refreshing sense of the truth. Unlike with politicians and bankers, there will be no doubletalk whatsoever. With that said, our country has reached an all-time low in our educational system and we, as a country, should be ashamed of ourselves. It's a disgrace that most of the American people, including most schoolteachers and college professors, do not know and/or understand what inflation really is, let alone the banking system that has been created within the United States. Therefore, the question that should be asked is why hasn't the teachers of our country been educated on the issues of inflation and banking? The answer is, for the most part, they themselves have also attended public schools, which appears to have an agenda on keeping the American people in the dark about inflation and banking. For that reason, let's take an active role in changing the perception of what the American people have been taught, if they were taught anything at all, which is nothing more than lies. To do so we will start with inflation. The true meaning of inflation has always been, at least it seemed to be, a secret that everyone was keeping from me. This would include my parents, friends, relatives, and even my teachers. In spite of all the lies, I was able to acquire the true definition of inflation and once I had done so I was very concerned. Furthermore, what I observed was, in fact, that most people did not know the true definition. I also found this to be extremely sad and very disappointing that no one, in my life at that time, knew the truth. They all resorted to speculation and rumors. Even though they had no clue as to the true definition they all believed they actually knew what the definition was. Everyone kept telling me that the definition of inflation is the increase in prices; however, my logical sense kept telling me that this was not the correct answer. Consequently, I had to study the issue of inflation on my own, which I encourage you to do the same. I, therefore, want to congratulate you for taking the first step in that direction, which is the reading of this book.

I truly believe that if more people understood the definition of inflation they would realize that it is not the increase in prices, but is actually the increase of the money supply. Even though inflation is the increase in available money, there are certain people that have artificially manipulated the American economy to increase the prices. They have done so by using the excuse of inflation. This is another deceptive tactic that has been implemented by the owners of the Federal Reserve Banks in order to control your wealth and ability to save, which we will get into in a moment. With this understanding we can truly see what they are doing to the purchasing power of our wealth and currency. By the time you reach the end of this chapter you will see that the result of inflation has been purposely created with the intent of stealing the wealth from the American people. You will also conclude that this process is one of the biggest illusions, outside of the personal Income Tax, that has ever been perpetrated against the American people.

For years, I couldn't understand how the Bankers, meaning the owners of the Federal Reserve Banks, could be getting away with there criminal act of robbing the American people and, more importantly, why were the American people allowing this to occur. Even though I was confused early on as to why this was occurring, I soon thereafter would be given the answer as to why. As stated before, the problem starts with the educational system and the actions taken by the treasonous bankers and government officials. Still, most people believe everything that is told to them by the news media, government officials, and financial experts, without questioning or confirming anything for themselves. This alone is heartbreaking, but we cannot assign blame to someone that does not inherently have the capability to understand the issues at hand. This, however, is not the case with someone who has chosen to remain complacent, lazy, and uninterested in protecting their fellow American's property and wealth. These types of individuals are absolutely a contributing factor and have betrayed their country and their fellow countrymen, but they are not to blame. Nevertheless, the blame should be shifted to who is responsible for perpetrating treason against the United States. Again, these individuals include the owners of the Federal Reserve Banks, the current and passed Chairmen of the Federal Reserve, and any government official that supports and/or continually justifies the illegal operations of the Fed and the U.S. Treasury, which includes the Internal Revenue Service. Furthermore, anyone who claims to be an expert in the area of economics and continually spreads falsehoods concerning our current system; like that of a public schoolteacher or college professor, is at more to blame. Why would I say such a thing? It's their responsibility to know the truth and to pass it on to the youth of America. If they, the teachers, do not know the truth then why are they teaching our children? This is where the problem begins. We should consider putting an end to the publicly subsidized educational system by allowing a private competitive system, which includes home schooling. These structures will do a much better job in educating our children correctly. To prove how bad the federally subsidized schools have become, all you have to do is open your eyes and look around. Again, it's in plain sight. As a person that had attended public school, I can attest to the fact that I did not learn how to read or write until two years after I graduated. So, you tell me. How can a student graduate from high school without having the ability to read or write? I can tell you, but that's another story.

Lets take a moment and look at a popular dictionary and see how it defines inflation. According to Webster's New Universal Unabridged Dictionary published in 1983, the second definition of "inflation" after "the act of inflating or the condition of being inflated" is:

> *"An increase in the amount of currency in circulation, resulting in a relatively sharp and sudden fall in its value and rise in prices: it may be caused by an increase in the volume of paper money issued or of gold mined, or a relative increase in expenditures as when the supply of goods fails to meet the demand."*

This definition touches on some of the basic aspects of inflation and would seem to indicate that inflation is not defined as the increase in prices, but is actually the increase in the supply of money. The increase in money causes the increase in prices; therefore, inflation is a cause of why prices increase. Another source, The American Heritage® Dictionary, defines Inflation as:

> *"A persistent increase in the level of consumer prices or a persistent decline in the purchasing power of money, caused by an increase in available currency and credit beyond the proportion of available goods and services."*

There's an interesting twist to the definition within the American Heritage's Dictionary compared to that of the Webster's version. Even though both of the definitions clearly state that prices rise due to an increase in available currency, the American Heritage definition published in 2000 has identified the result of inflation first. This is illogical and would just confuse the average person as to what the true definition of inflation really is. At this point in time, the American Heritage Dictionary has successfully put the cart before the horse. Somewhere between the 1980s and the year 2000 the definition appears to have shifted from the cause to the result. Common sense tells us that if you inflate an object like a balloon or a currency in a monetary system you have to introduce more of what was already present. When inflation is referred to, for monetary purposes, the introduction of more currency is the act of inflating the economy, not the increase in prices. Now, for clarification purposes, you must keep in mind that there is a huge difference between inflation and that of supply and demand. Prices also increase due to supply and demand, which occurs when supply is limited. However, when prices rise due to inflation[28], which is the increase in available currency, that's nothing more than a man-made illusion and a secret tax, period! Again, I have used the word illusion and I have now called inflation a secret tax. I say this because inflation, as it is occurring today, does not truly exist, that is outside of supply and demand. With that said, another question that needs to be asked is, why do prices go up just because the demand is greater than the supply? Well, there are only two main reasons why this would happen. The first is greediness, which has consequences once it has been revealed. The second is an inconvenience that was placed upon the supplier. I can prove this without going into great detail. Have you ever mailed a package using Federal Express or UPS and requested that your package be sent next business day? I know I have and I've paid a lot more than

---

[28] Inflation Defined - "An increase in the amount of currency in circulation, resulting in a relatively sharp and sudden fall in its value and rise in prices: it may be caused by an increase in the volume of paper money issued or of gold mined, or a relative increase in expenditures as when the supply of goods fails to meet the demand." *Webster's New Universal Unabridged Dictionary*.

the standard rate for normal delivery. Better yet, here's another scenario. Lets say that you are selling doghouses right before winter and you only have 2 available; however, at the same time you have 20 customers wanting one. You may be a greedy person and will exploit the situation by charging your customers more for the remaining two doghouses, which could very well result in having upset customers. Or, in fact, you have promised to deliver 18 more doghouses within one week's time, which due to the inconvenience has resulted in a higher price being set. Even though you may have set a higher price your customers have been satisfied. You see it's quite simple. Due to the time constraint being placed on you in the construction of the additional doghouses, which had been agreed on by your customers, this in itself warrants a higher price. This, however, has nothing to do with greediness. Still, you have to keep in mind that the terms of the agreement have been entered into voluntarily; therefore, the construction will begin. So, as you can see, the price of the doghouses has increased due to supply and demand, but it had nothing to do with inflation, which is the increase of available currency. Furthermore, as you may have noticed, the price of the existing doghouses did not increase just because you had a short supply. The point I am trying to make is that there is no need for the price of an existing product to increase. Therefore, the price of an existing item, that already had its cost calculated within the existing price, would only increase because the owner of said item would be showing themselves as and immoral and greedy person.

The important point to take note of is that inflation and the increase in prices that we are experiencing today is not, as some would believe, a natural occurrence. It is; therefore, nothing more than a man-made illusion. The purpose of this illusion is to fool the American people into believing that the increase in prices is an inevitable outcome to the printing of more money. This; however, is not the case and it couldn't be further from the truth. Today's inflationary effect is nothing more than a hidden tax and, more importantly, is a hidden tactic that is being used to legally extract the wealth from the majority of the American people. Just like in a dictatorship, wherein such a person claiming to be the dictator has to create and maintain an illusion that he or she is the sole person in control, because the dictatorship doesn't really exist. No one person can run an entire country; therefore, they will have to have a team of people to assist them. This fact contradicts the meaning of a dictatorship. When most people refer to inflation they are referring to it in the same manner as they would refer to a dictatorship. They are not referring to its true nature. Just because someone refers to a dolphin as a fish does not make a dolphin a fish. The same is true with inflation when it is referred to as the increase in prices. This is why the creators of this tactic have to keep the truth, concerning their artificial increase in prices, a secret. For if they did not, the American people would know that they are being lied to and stolen from. On the other hand, some people know that inflation is the increase in the money supply; however, they continue to believe that this is the reason why prices increase. Therefore, I must ask, why do they believe such a thing? If you believe that prices increase as a result of inflation, which means there is more money available to purchase the same amount of goods, I only have one question. Even though, on its surface, inflation seems like a good explanation as to why prices increase today; however, why would prices increase when no one in the private sector knows how much money is in circulation?

Can you see how a simple question will open up an avenue for the truth to be revealed? When it concerns inflation and why prices increase, no one knows how much money is in circulation, at least outside of the owners of the Federal Reserve Banks. With that said, here's another question. If no one knows exactly how much money is in circulation, including the people within the Federal government, why would the value of the dollar lose its purchasing power just because there's more of it? More importantly, why would private companies want the cost of their products to increase, which will result in a decrease in the amount of sales? As I see it, if it were not for the owners of the Federal Reserve Banks telling businesses to increase their prices the American people would just be wealthier. Some people, for whatever reason, have a difficult time understanding this argument. Therefore, I suggest that we take a moment and reflect on the history of our country. Before the year of 1933, when our country's money was gold and silver, if you had discovered more gold or silver the prices of everyday items did not necessarily increase. If anything, you would have become wealthier because you were the person that had found the precious metal. This is true for one main reason. No one person within our country would have known how much gold or silver was in circulation. However, unlike years ago, in today's market there is an entity that knows how much money they have printed and, therefore, due to their over printing they have a need to deceive the American people. Why would they have such a need to deceive? They, the owners of the Federal Reserve Banks, know that they have created an enormous amount of money which will effectively allow the American people to become wealthier and; therefore, the owners of these banks would lose their control over the people. In no way will they allow this to occur. Therefore, our current system has been altered, from its original design and intent, so that a few immoral, greedy, and corrupt individuals will have the ability to control the American people by stealing their wealth through the means of deliberately decreasing the purchasing power of their money and wealth. This is being accomplished by purposely and artificially increasing the cost of goods, thus the illusion. Once the bankers had successfully, with the help of the Federal government, implemented the illusionary inflation rate, the owners of the Federal Reserve Banks knew that they would have their secret tax.

Now that you are aware of the true definition of inflation, I must pose a very important question at this juncture. In order to ask the question I must lay down the foundation for asking it. As you may know, certain Congressmen, along with the chairman of the

Federal Reserve, Ben Bernanke, have periodically admitted that the current inflation rate according to the M3 report[29], Consumer Price Index, and the Producer Price Index is approximately 12 to 16 percent. What does this mean? This means that you are currently losing anywhere between 12 to 16 percent of the purchasing power of your money and/or wealth that you have created. This includes the currency that you have chosen to exchange for your labor. Now remember, some would say that this is due to the Federal Reserve Banks creating more dollars every day. This; however, is not, in any way, the whole truth. The owners of the Federal Reserve Banks are controlling the American people by deliberately increasing overall prices, as mentioned earlier. Some of the tools that they are using consist of the reports like that of the CPI and PPI. Nevertheless, if you are not earning at least 16 percent or more on your money you are losing a substantial amount of your wealth. With that said, is it okay for a criminal to come into your home, point a gun at you, and steal 16 percent of your wealth? No, it's not okay. So why is it okay that the governments of our country, along with the Federal Reserve Banks, are allowed to do virtually the same thing? Has it now become acceptable for the Federal, State, and local governments, which includes the private corporation of the Federal Reserve Banks, to involve themselves in the criminal act of theft and robbery? I hope that you would say no. If so, why is it that the American people keep justifying the Feds' criminal behavior? Is it okay that a government entity can spend irresponsibly and then hold you responsible for the repayment of their debt? Please tell me it's not so! If you believe otherwise, consider this. For the most part, the American people have been deceived into believing that their actions are not theft. Could this be true because the Federal Reserve does not directly send out agents to commit acts of theft or extortion,

---

[29] M3 – The M3 was a report published by the Federal Reserve Banks, which indicated the amount of money created, and supplied to the Federal government. The Federal Reserve Banks ceased publishing the M3 statistics in March of 2006.

all at the point of a gun? Wait a second; they do! They indeed have agents that are sent out into the public sector in order to steal from the American people. The agents that are sent out to conduct these unlawful practices consist of and represent departments like that of the IRS, BATF, and, disturbingly enough, the local Sheriff's Departments. Not only do they steal your wealth directly; they also commit the acts of theft and extortion indirectly, by the use of illusionary and deceptive tactics. Furthermore, make no mistake, they will arrive with guns and; sadly enough, they are willing to use them against their fellow Americans, that's to say they are Americans themselves. Still, these agents are sent out into the so-called free States with an objective. Their objective is to threaten, rob, and extort from the American people, which in some cases may result in the murder of their victims. This is being implemented in the same manner as Mafia families did years ago. The sad part about all of this is that they are getting away with committing multiple crimes. If you and I were to do what these agencies are doing today, we would go to prison for the rest of our natural lives. So, again, how can this be acceptable? Nevertheless, the owners of the Federal Reserve Banks are in charge and will use whatever tactics they feel is necessary to complete their objective, even if that objective involves criminal behavior. The reason why the owners of the Federal Reserve Banks are getting away with their unjust and unlawful acts is due to the fact that most of the American population is unaware that these malicious crimes are being committed. It's time to wake up and start asking questions.

In the past, the Federal Reserve Banks used to supply the Federal government with a report called the M3, which reported the amount of Federal Reserve Notes that had been created. In spite of this requirement, the Federal Reserve Banks have taken it upon themselves to no longer supply this report to the Federal government and, more importantly, to Congress. So, again, if no one knows, that is outside of the bankers themselves, how much currency is actually in existence this should prove that the increase in prices is being artificially created without any regard to the people's hard work, savings, or their well being. The proof has always been in plain sight. Therefore, if you were to conduct some research you will find that prices really do not increase at all, unless there is a shortage of a certain product. Just use gold and silver as your medium, during your research, and the truth will be revealed.

In a free market, with no restrictions to competition, prices of goods always fall and the quality of the same product increases. Opposed to a totally free market, just like what is happening today, there are three main reasons why the price of an item will increase. This is especially true in a heavily regulated market, which limits competition. Only one of these three reasons is a natural occurrence and we already know what that is. It is the natural occurrence of supply and demand. Supply and demand always plays a role on prices in any market, free or not. However, the other two remaining reasons, which would cause prices to increase, are not natural occurrences and are purposely created. They are described as inflation and government regulation. Inflation and government regulations are anything but a natural occurrence and were created to deceive the American people. There is no arguing the fact that both of these affect the economy and, as a result, increase prices. They were purposely created to extract the wealth from the American people and to redistribute whatever is remaining, which in itself is socialism. Nevertheless, when a currency of value is used, like that of gold and silver, along with the introduction of technology prices always fall or remain the same. This can be proven easily without much effort. Just take a look at the electronics industry and, more importantly, take a look at what Henry Ford had accomplished with his assembly line. Contrary to popular belief, Henry Ford was not the first person to build a practical automobile. He, however, knew what the people wanted and was able to deliver it. Henry Ford stated, "I will build a car for the great multitude" and created the Model T in 1908. Henry Ford's Model T was the first automobile to be mass-produced by an assembly line and Henry

Ford introduced all of the techniques that were used. This resulted in the model T's price dropping from approximately $850 in 1908 to just under $300 in 1925. This fact in history proves, beyond a shadow of a doubt, that creativity and technology in a free market, with little to no government involvement, will always result in a higher output of production, more jobs, and lower prices. If you remember anything, remember this. It is a fact that prices have increased over the years, but not because there is more money in circulation, which is supposedly the reason why the purchasing power of the currency has fallen. Overall prices, along with the amount of money, have increased because the owners of the Federal Reserve Banks say they do. It really is that simple! These individuals determine how much money will be created and as to what the current prices of goods should be. This, in itself, is the illusion. With that said, I should explain. The owners of the Federal Reserve Banks use their banks and their influential name to force the producers of products to increase their prices by the issuance of certain reports namely the GDP (gross domestic product), the PPI (producer price index), and the CPI (consumer price index). Again, this is purposely orchestrated in order to remove our wealth without us knowing it. Before 1933 and 1965 we, as a country, used gold and silver as our currency. Therefore, inflation was basically non-existent. Still, over the last one hundred years, we have somehow veered from the Law, which requires the use of real money. The Law describes a true dollar as a measurement of gold and silver. There are two ways to prove this statement. The first is to look up the legal definition of what a dollar means. The second is to purchase a one-ounce silver dollar, with the paper "dollars" that you are using today. Once you have obtained the silver dollar, read what is written on the coin. It reads, "United States of America 1 oz. Fine Silver One Dollar". If the coin is not truly a dollar then why does it claim to be one dollar? Have you ever heard the phrase, "our money used to be backed by gold and silver"? Well, you're in for a surprise. That is a big fat lie! Our money was never backed by gold and silver, our money WAS gold and silver.

Still, some people say that the population is too large today and that's why we don't use gold and silver. When asked as to why they would make such a statement they reply by stating, "There isn't enough to go around." This is an absurd statement to make, which reveals a person's ignorance. Why would I make such a claim? Well, again, it's quite simple. Let me give you a similarity in how this would work. Remember, the ownership of gold and silver would work in the same manner as the ownership of a company's stock. When stock of a company has become highly popular, its value has been increased to an unusual amount, and the demand of such stock has increased the stock will split. This means that you have just double the amount of your wealth, that is to say that you had ownership of said stock before the split had occurred. This is why the Law states that; "The Congress shall have the power to coin money, regulate the value thereof... ...and fix the Standards of Weights and Measures." Even though these facts are in plain sight, some people, to my disbelief, continually state that prices are going up due to the increase in the population. Again, no one should believe such a statement because we are not experiencing a shortage of any item, other than money itself. To prove this, are we experiencing a shortage of food, clothing, or automobiles? No, we are not; therefore, such a statement is absurd. If anything, there are more clothes, food, and automobiles available today then ever before. In addition, if the manufacturer's success of said items were truly dependent on them conducting their business correctly they would have learned how to produce these items for less than what it cost back in the 1940s and 1960s. With today's technology and the increase in efficiency of production the price of any product should decrease, not increase! It is easier, faster, and would be cheaper to manufacture an automobile today if it were not for the interference of the Federal government with its regulations. Therefore, we can now account for the two main reasons why the costs of certain items continue to increase today. Again, these two elements consist of the deliberate manipulation of the purchasing power of the currency and government regulations, which unjustly adds underlining costs to any product. As you can see, the best way to enslave a free and voluntary society, which has an open and competitive economy, is to regulate its industries heavily and to destroy their currency. The Federal Reserve Banks, along with the U.S. Congress, have done an outstanding job in accomplishing both, which is destroying the American economy and is enslaving the American people as a whole.

The Fed – The Horrible Truth

Okay, are you still with me? Good. Don't let the title of this section scare you off, because it's really important and actually quite simple to understand. I'm going to do my best to make this as easy as possible. As I am writing this section, I know that I have to cover this topic as quickly as possible, because I only have a few minutes before most people become completely bored of this subject. If I have offended you with that statement I apologize. With that said, I will guarantee that if you skip this section you will not be able to see the truth as to what is happening to us and to our beloved country. Therefore, you will now be enlightened.

Are you ready? Here we go…

> *"If the American people ever allowed private banks to control the issue of their currency, first by inflation and then by deflation, the banks and the corporations that will grow up around them will deprive the people of all property until their children will wake up homeless on the continent their fathers conquered."-Thomas Jefferson*

You must admit, that is a good quote. Therefore, I had to slip it in. If you can remember this quote while you read this chapter you will see what Thomas Jefferson was talking about. Therefore, lets get right to it. In an interview with Jim Lehrer, Alan

Greenspan admitted that the Federal Reserve, which includes the 12 regional banks, is not a government agency. This should put to rest any doubts as to the status of the Federal Reserve Banks and should quiet the ignorant individuals that blindly believe any information that is put out by the governments of our country. Furthermore, when asked by Jim Lehrer as to what should be the proper relationship between a chairman of the Fed and The President of the United States Alan Greenspan said:

> *"Well, first of all, the Federal Reserve is an independent agency and that means, basically, that there is no other agency of government which can overrule actions that we take. So long as that is in place and there is no evidence that the administration or the Congress or anybody else is requesting that we do things other than what we think is the appropriate thing, then what the relationships are don't frankly matter."-Alan Greenspan*

Just in case you are not aware, "The Fed" is short for the Federal Reserve System or, more importantly, it can be used to describe the Federal Reserve Banks[30] within the Federal Reserve System. I say this because the Federal Reserve System and I must emphasize "SYSTEM" is part of the Federal government. However, there is a hidden secret concerning the 12 regional banks, which are referred to as the Federal Reserve Banks. The Federal Reserve "SYSTEM" only oversees these 12 regional banks. Some would say that this makes these 12 regional banks quasi-government. However, that couldn't be further from the truth. Quasi[31], just in case you didn't know, is a Latin term that means "as if". Sadly enough, this is a term that some people use to justify something that

---

[30] Federal Reserve Banks – There are 12 regional Federal Reserve Banks throughout the United States. *The Federal Reserve System.*

[31] Quasi - Latin for as if, seemingly, but not actually; in some sense; resembling; nearly. *Black's Law dictionary seventh edition.*

they cannot or do not understand, especially those that have found their way into a government position. Somewhere throughout their career they became aware of this word and, with its use, they believe they can answer a question with an untruth. With that said, I'll give you an example. Let's say I work for Lockheed Martin, at Goddard Space Flight Center NASA, and you were to ask me where do I work. I could simply say that I work at NASA and, for all intents and purposes, I am a quasi-federal government employee. On the contrary, the truth is that I'm not. The truth is that I work for a private corporation, not for the Federal government. Therefore, just because I work at NASA does not make me a Federal government employee. Even though this is true, most people find it hard to believe that the 12 regional banks are not part of the Federal government. Well, surprise! The truth is that the Federal Reserve Banks, which are within the Federal Reserve System, are independently owned and operated. That's right, the 12 regional banks are NOT part of the Federal government. Some people are surprised to hear this. Still, most people say that they had their suspicions or they already knew that the banks are privately owned. In any case, I commend you for taking the time to learn the truth about these 12 regional banks and what they are doing to our beloved country. However, before going forward, we must address this allegation. For if we do not address the allegation concerning these banks we all know that it will remain just that, an allegation. Therefore, in order to prove or disprove this allegation all one needs to do is research the Fed itself.

The U.S. Government Printing Office sells books on this subject and within some of these publications there are diagrams that articulate the structure of the Fed and the 12 privately owned banks. I have purchased a few of these books and I am going to address two of them here. The titles of these two books are, "The Federal Reserve System, Purposes & Functions", Library of Congress card number 39-26719, and "A Primer on the Fed, Federal Reserve Bank of Richmond" by Alfred Broaddus. While both of these books are great tools for information about the Federal Reserve Banks and their operations, I'm only going to quote a couple of small sections from each. The first is the book titled, "A Primer on the Fed". Initially, this book appears to be referencing the Bank of Richmond Virginia. However, on page 17 it talks about the 12 regional banks and as to how many banks there are, their locations, and their functions. First, let's make it clear for the record as to where these banks are located. The following locations of the 12 Banks and their respective cities are; Boston, New York, Philadelphia, Cleveland, Richmond, Atlanta, Chicago, St Louis, Minneapolis, Kansas City, Dallas, and San Francisco. Now that we know the locations, let's go into the structure, if you will. According to this book, on page 17, it states:

> *"As suggested earlier, the Federal Reserve Banks represent the more decentralized and private elements of the Fed's overall structure."*

We have to stop here and address this. Do you see how they are using the word "Fed" to describe the overall system? And, were you aware that the Federal Reserve System consisted of private elements and that these private elements were the Federal Reserve Banks? It went on to read:

> *"The corporate structure of the Federal Reserve Banks is similar to that of private commercial banks. Like private banks, each reserve Bank has a board of directors consisting of private individuals, elects the bank's officers and oversees the general operation of the bank. The banks also issue capital stock, and their officers carry titles similar to those used in most private financial institutions."*

Is it by any chance starting to walk like a duck and quack like a duck? Nevertheless, this is where it gets good.

> " *While similar to private companies in these respects,*
> *however, the Federal Reserve Banks are different in many*
> *other, fundamental respects. First, because the banks*
> *principal general responsibility is to promote the public*
> *interest rather than the narrower interests of their*
> *stockholders, profit considerations do not play a dominant*
> *role in determining the bank's actions, even though the*
> *banks earned substantial profits as a byproduct of their*
> *routine operations."*

This is no joke! Can you believe what they wrote? If you didn't get it, read it again. I'll summarize in a minute; however, I must first quote from the second book titled "The Federal Reserve System, Purposes and Functions".

> *"The Federal Reserve supplies reserves to the banking*
> *system in two ways; Lending through the Federal Reserve*
> *discount window, and buying government securities."*

As you can see, the Federal Reserve Banks are just like private corporations and privately owned commercial banks. They even have a Board of Directors that consist of private individuals, not government officials. These banks also issue capital stock, just like any other private corporation. Then they try to use doubletalk by saying, "while similar to private companies... ...the Federal Reserve Banks are different". They want us to believe that they are looking in the best interest of the American people, while their primary focus is on the best interest of their stockholders and their responsibility in promoting the Federal Reserve System to the public. Well, guess what? They have to, because if the American people truly understood this fraud they would abolish it. They go on to say, that profit considerations do not play a dominant role. When I read this statement I asked myself, did the author really state that making a profit is not a dominant role for these independent companies? Who does he think he is fooling and, more importantly, who does he think will be reading this material? That's the main goal of every company. Without profit, they wouldn't be able to function. Oh, that's right. They don't need to make a profit, because they have the authority to create their profit from the printing press or by a keystroke on a computer. What is even weirder is that the author would want you to believe that these banks do not make it a priority to make a profit, but rather the "substantial profits" that are obtained should be considered "as a byproduct of their routine operations". Again, you have to be kidding me. His statement is flat out double talk. The truth can be clearly seen for what it is. Still, they want us to believe that the banks do not make earning a profit a priority. This is just nonsense.

This next piece of information is very important and interesting to say the least. The Federal Reserve supplies reserves to the banking system in two ways. The first way is by lending it into circulation. The second way is by buying government securities. This is what they would want you to believe but the secondary source is nothing more than another way to lend the funds into circulation. Even though it appears that there are two separate ways for money to come into existence that is nothing more than another illusionary tactic. In fact, there is only one way. The banks create the money, which we use today, by lending it out. There is no other way for money to come into existence within our country. Consequently, when the Federal Reserve Banks buy government securities the government is borrowing money and then is required to repay the principal along with the interest. This also applies to you when you have decided to buy a government bond or security. You're buying them as an investment. Therefore, the government has to pay you interest in addition to the principle. The only difference between you buying a government security and that of the Federal Reserve Banks is that you have to exchange your hard earned money in order to buy the security. The owners of the Federal Reserve Banks are only required to sign a check or press a few keys on a keyboard and with that action they magically have their money to buy the government securities. Now, is that fair?

"The dollar represents a one dollar debt to the Federal Reserve system. The Federal Reserve Banks create money out of thin air to buy government bonds from the U.S. Treasury... ... thus creating out of nothing a debt, which the American people are obligated to pay with interest." Congressman, Wright Patman

Let's take it a step further and go into some legal evidence that again proves the allegation that the Federal Reserve Banks are not part of the Federal government. I must draw your attention to a few court cases that proves this fact. I'll try to keep out most of the legalese, so as not to bore you. Here are the court cases and their site, if you're interested in reading them for yourself:

SCOTT v. FEDERAL RESERVE BANK OF KANSAS CITY, et al., Appellee. No. 04-2357. 406 F.3d 532 United States Court of Appeals, Eighth Circuit.

The Bank argues that it is not a federal agency for purposes of Rule 4 because Federal Reserve Banks are distinct from the Board of Governors, owned by commercial banks, and directly supervised in their daily operations by separate boards of directors — not the federal government. Further, the Bank states that Federal Reserve Bank employees are not considered federal employees, officials, or representatives for purposes of 12 U.S.C. § 341. The Bank also contends, inter alia, that the plain language of 28 U.S.C. § 451 and relevant case law state that Federal Reserve Banks are not federal agencies.

...persons other than the government have a proprietary interest in the Federal Reserve Banks. Federal Reserve Banks are not listed as either wholly-owned or mixed-ownership corporations under federal law. 31 U.S.C. § 9101. Instead, individual commercial member banks own stock in Federal Reserve Banks and elect a majority (six out of nine) of each bank's board of directors.

> *Accordingly, although entities other than the federal government have a proprietary interest in the Federal Reserve Banks, this factor also demonstrates the government's interest in the Federal Reserve Banks.*

This last paragraph is very disturbing. How would you feel if the banker told you, when you went and purchased your home, that there are undisclosed persons that will be holding the majority of interest in your property and at their discretion can do whatever they want at their will? However, you shouldn't worry about anything because you still "own" the property. Would you believe that horse crap? I hope you wouldn't. Really I do! Come on, does the government think that we are so stupid that we will believe whatever they tell us so long as it comes from them. Is this the purpose of their public school system? To train us so that we will ignore the facts even though they are flaunting them right in front of our faces? It reminds me of a time when I was at an administrative hearing, helping a friend of mine, and got into a debate with an attorney about the word "and" and as to what it means. Yes, as silly as it sounds, the word "and" came up as a debate. I would not have believed it if it had not happened to me. Again, my apologies for getting off track, so lets move ahead and examined the rest of the cases. This next case is fairly recent. It was decided in 1999 and it's very interesting to say the least. Pay close attention to the wording and the truth will reveal itself.

COHEN v. EMPIRE BLUE CROSS and BLUE SHIELD, 176 F.3d 35, 42 (2d Cir.1999).

> *...no statute designates Federal Reserve Banks as federal agencies. Federal Reserve Banks are authorized to be government fiscal agents... However, the Second Circuit, has held that acting as an agent for the government does not make that entity a federal agency.*

Here's a side note. If there's no statute, there can be no law. That's pretty easy to understand, wouldn't you agree.

LEWIS v. UNITED STATES, 680 F.2d 1239 (1982) No. 80-5905 United States Court of Appeals, Ninth Circuit:

Plaintiff, who was injured by a vehicle owned and operated by a Federal Reserve Bank, brought action- alleging jurisdiction under the Federal Tort Claims Act. The United States District Court for the Central District of California, David W. Williams, J., dismissed the case, holding that Federal Reserve Bank was not a Federal agency *within meaning of Act and that the court therefore lacked subject-matter jurisdiction. Appeal was taken. The Court of Appeals, Poole, Circuit Judge, held that Federal Reserve Banks are not Federal* instrumentalities *for purposes of the Act, but are independent, privately owned and locally controlled corporations.*

The court went on to say:

"...the Federal Reserve Banks are not Federal instrumentalities for purposes of a Federal Tort Claims Act, but are independent, privately owned and locally controlled corporations in light of fact that direct supervision and control of each bank is exercised by board of directors, Federal Reserve Banks, though heavily regulated, are locally controlled by their member banks, banks are listed neither as "wholly owned" government corporations nor as "mixed ownership" corporations; Federal Reserve Banks receive no appropriated funds from Congress and the banks are empowered to sue and be sued in their own names..."

Here's additional proof. This is what the assistant of the board of governors of the Federal Reserve System had to say:

"The Federal Reserve System pays the U.S. Treasury $20.60 per thousand of Federal Reserve Notes [which are

U.S. dollars] ... a little over two cents each ... without regard to the face value of the note. Federal Reserve notes, incidentally, are the only type of currency now produced for circulation. They are printed exclusively by the Treasurer's Bureau of engraving and printing, and the $20.60 per thousand price reflects the bureau's full cost of production. Federal Reserve notes are printed in 1, 2, 5, 10, 20, 50, and $100 denominations only notes of 500, 1000, 5000, and 10,000 denominations were last printed in 1945." Donald J. Winn, assistant to the Board of Governors of the Federal Reserve System

There may be numerous questions that arise out of this quote, but there are only two that need to be asked. That's if you still believe that the Federal Reserve Banks are part of the Federal government. First, why is it that the Federal Reserve System pays the U.S. Treasury $20.60 per 1000 notes. If the Federal Reserve System, more specifically the banks within the system, were part of the Federal government then why would the Federal Reserve Banks be paying the government? Worded differently, why would the government be paying itself? I know that he said that the Federal Reserve System pays the U.S. Treasury, but we all know that if it weren't for the 12 regional banks there would be no system. Therefore, we are directed into the second question. Who is actually paying the $20.60? The answer is that it's the 12 regional Federal Reserve Banks. Again, with that said, wouldn't it be safe to say that when the Federal Reserve System pays the U.S. Treasury it is in essence paying itself, that's if the Federal Reserve Banks are part of the Federal government? Therefore, if this were to be the truth then why would the government have to borrow money and pay interest to these banks, which is owned by the government? It would make absolutely no logical sense whatsoever. Therefore, this proves that these banks are privately owned and operated. If, for some reason, you still believe their lies you are doing so for one reason only. That is because these banks have the word federal in their name. If this is the case, are you familiar with a company called Federal Express? Does this make Federal Express, or FedEx for short, part of the Federal government? No, it does not. If you're getting upset, please remember that you are doing so because, at this point, you are running straight off of emotion. However, I understand how it feels to have your belief system undermined, because it happened to me. It feels like your foundation is falling down from underneath you, but it doesn't change the fact that this is true. There is no disputing the fact that the Federal Reserve Banks are privately owned and operated. In more support, there is an easier way to prove that the Federal Reserve Banks are not part of the Federal government. All you have to do is open your telephone book and you will see that the Federal Reserve Banks are not listed in the blue pages where all of the other Federal government agencies are listed, they're listed in the white pages next to Federal Express. Now, is there any doubt as to the Federal Reserve Banks being a privately owned corporation? Still, who are the owners of the Federal Reserve Banks? Well, we'll come back to that question.

Okay, that's it for the Fed's structure. Are you still with me? Good. Way to go, you're hanging tough. In summary, we have the Federal Reserve System, which is part of the Federal government and that system has been setup to govern the 12 privately owned banks. That's simple to understand, isn't it? I told you this would be easy. Anyhow, now that we have the structure behind us, here's where the rubber meets the road. Understanding this next issue is actually quite simple, if explained in simple terms. In order to do that, I must first ask you a few questions. Let's start with; do you have an outstanding loan on your vehicle? If your answer is yes then you have, as some would call it, a car note[32]? Meaning, you are currently making payments on your automobile to another party.

---

[32] Note defined – n. 1. A written promise by one party to pay money to another party or to bearer - also termed a promissory note. *Blacks Law Dictionary Seventh Edition*

Okay, now that the first question is out of the way and, hopefully, you are starting to understand what a note is. Here's the second question. Do you owe any money to a friend, family member, or even to a financial institution? Again, if your answer is yes, then you have a promissory note. As you can see, with just asking a few questions, we can now safely say that we understand what a note is. A note is a promise to pay another and it represents debt. In addition, once the borrower (you) and the lender (the "note holder") create the note, can the "note holder" sell their interest in the note? The answer is yes and, more importantly; this is extremely common in home mortgages. And yes, home mortgages are notes as well. I knew you were going to ask that question. Are you still with me? I hope that you are. This is where most people become amazed. Get your wallet or purse and take out a dollar bill, that's if you have one. I don't care if it's a five, ten, or a twenty. If you don't have one, get a hold of one. Once you have the dollar bill, go to the very top of it and read what it says. If I'm not mistaken it reads "Federal Reserve Note". Was I correct? Does your dollar bill read Federal Reserve Note at the top? You're probably saying yes, but so what? Some would say that there's nothing wrong with having notes as currency; however, I would strongly oppose such statement. Furthermore, even though some may disagree, we as a country have used notes before the Federal Reserve Notes of today. Abraham Lincoln was the first president to create and use such a currency. It was commonly known as the greenback. However, the true name of this note was not the greenback, it is the United States Note. President Kennedy continued the use of the United States Note all the way up to his assassination. How do I know this to be true? Outside of researching this issue, I own a few of the previously printed United States Notes. Therefore, you may be asking yourself, what is the difference between these two notes? Well, in simple terms, the difference between a Federal Reserve Note and that of the United States Note is that the government owns the United States Note, which would affectively abolish the interest being charged for the use of the Federal Reserve Notes, which is owned by a private corporation. If we were still using gold and silver as our money or even the United States Note there would be no interest to repay back to these crooked bankers. Yes, I said crooked bankers.

> *"You are a den of vipers and thieves. I intend to route you out, and by the eternal God, I will route you out... if people only understood the rank injustice of the money and banking system, there would be a revolution by morning." President Andrew Jackson*

Who, in their right mind, believes that it is okay for the government to borrow a currency, which they themselves could make on their own, and then be required to repay the debt with interest? Again, does this make any sense? No, it does not, especially when the Federal government can just create the money itself, even though it is Constitutionally incorrect. Why would I suggest such a thing? It appears that the government doesn't care about the Constitution anyway, so why not have the government go back to creating there own money in order to remove these elite bankers from power. Nevertheless, as stated before, this is not a new idea. Therefore, when the government had created the United States Note, which served as a legal tender, they did NOT have to pay any interest on that type of currency? Why? The currency, of that time, belonged to the American people and not to a private corporation. I could get into more in-depth about this subject, but that's not the purpose of this book. This book is intended to peek your interest and to expose the truth of what's happening to America today. You have to keep one thing in mind, if we do not come together and do something our children and our grandchildren will have to repay this debt or pay this price for our stupidity, cowardliness, or stubbornness.

You can relax now; you've made it through the hardest part. Way to go! I congratulate you and want you to know that it's all down hill from here. This is the part that exposes the fraud that has been perpetrated on the American people. With that said, I'll cover this quickly. Contrary to popular belief, the debt that Congress has accumulated can never be paid off or paid back, whichever way you would like to say it. It's easy to understand once you recognize this simple and straightforward fact. The debt cannot be paid back in the same currency in which it was borrowed. I'm going to prove it, here and now. In order to prove this you and I must engage in a bit of role-playing, at least for a minute or two. I hope that you're willing to play. If you've made it this far, I believe you are. Therefore, we need to create the scenario. You represent the entire Federal government and I, on the other hand, represent the 12 regional Federal Reserve banks, which I own inclusively. In 1913 you created a law, the Federal Reserve Act, which allows me to create money out of thin air and, coincidently, that same year I mandated that you create and pass the Internal Revenue Act as well. I'll explain the reason for the Internal Revenue Act in a moment. Nevertheless, let's continue. You're the Federal government and I am the Federal Reserve Bank. You now have given me the authority to create my own money called the Federal Reserve Note. At this point, I have only created 10 dollars and you want to borrow all of them. I agree with your request and want to lend them to you at 10 percent interest for one year. You agree with the terms and; therefore, you borrowed the ten dollars. This is where it begins to get interesting. Since you have borrowed the first and only $10 that I Have created, which you are being charged 10% interest, how much are you going to owe at the end of the year? Well, let's take a look at this. 10% of $10 is $1, correct? So, with the interest of $1 and the principle of $10 that comes to a total amount due of $11. Now remember, I as the Federal Reserve Bank have only created $10. Therefore, where are you going to get the other dollar to repay the interest that you owe me? The answer is, it's not available. I haven't created any more currency as of yet, outside of the original $10 that you had borrowed. Therefore, you'll have to come back and borrow another $10, which I'll create out of thin air, in order for you to repay your first debt. You will now have to take one dollar from the second loan in order to satisfy the first loan. Even though you have satisfied the first loan, you are now two dollars short in order to repay the second loan. Consequently, by the end of the next year you'll be two dollars short. By the third year you'll be three dollars short and so on. Are you getting the picture yet? That's it! I told you it would be easy to understand.

Still, I told you that I would explain the mandate for the Income Tax. The mandate for the Income Tax Act is that the owners of the Federal Reserve Bank knew that the officials within Washington D.C. would default on their obligations to repay their loans and that this Act would ensure some type of repayment. The interesting part is that the bankers knew that any borrower would eventually have to default on their obligations. How did they know this? They knew it because they intentionally setup the system in such a way to ensure bankruptcies or defaults. This is why they created bankruptcy laws. This is nothing more than a criminal activity made legal. Nonetheless, its intention and how it is written today does not give any government the authority to tax the American people, the human beings, directly. It's only intention, which has not changed, as according to the law, is to tax corporations and their profits and nonresident aliens, which are foreigners. What does this mean? It means that nonresident foreigners and fictitious and/or legal entities are liable for this type of tax. Why is this? It would be illegal, even currently today, for any government to forcibly take an American person's property without first offering them due process of law. The 5th Amendment guarantees this right and was created for this specific purpose, as to prevent the governments of our country from arbitrarily taking someone's property without an opportunity to be heard. Does this sound familiar? This illegal act is happening today with the IRS. Still, why is it that some States and the Federal government can tax a corporation and foreign person, but not an American person residing within the borders of the United States of America? The answer is simple. The Constitution does not apply to or afford protections to corporations (domestic corporation or foreign corporation) or non-resident aliens (a foreigner that resides in another country). All one has to do, in order to prove this, is to read the law. Not only will you find this to be true, you will also see that when an American goes outside this country to work they themselves become liable for the payment of the Income Tax. Again, however, they get a high amount of their earned income exempted from this liability. Most of the American people are being taxed on their labor and/or income as if they are working outside of this country and are not afforded the same exemption amount. How wrong is this? Due to the misapplication of the tax laws, this has and will continue to encourage employers to send jobs overseas and employees to look for work outside of our country. When the governments of our country, including that of local authorities, imposes or enforces a direct tax, such as that of the Income Tax, on an American Citizen they have broken the law and have engaged themselves in the act of extortion. Most of the American people know this to be true, but yet do nothing. Let me make it perfectly clear, when it concerns the American people the current law is being misapplied. Some would even say that it is un-constitutional. I, however, believe differently. I find it to be Constitutional; however, it is being misapplied to the innocent hard working people, which is the backbone of America. The only problem, which is an inconsistency with the foundation of our country, is that the implementation of this law is incorrect and that it can in no way be mandatory. Even though it is voluntary, as stated before, the sad part is that most of the American people have been tricked into signing two documents that appear to have made them liable for such a tax. The first is the Social Security Application and the second is the Tax Return itself.

Therefore, all direct taxes, passed by the Federal government, are to be placed upon the States and their property like land, real estate, and corporate profit, not upon the people. All direct taxes must be apportioned[33], meaning distributed proportionately, among all the 50 States. A direct tax placed upon the people directly is only authorized once Congress has declared War, which has a two-year restriction. This two-year restriction limits the government from taxing the people directly for an indefinite amount of time. At that point, once voted on, they could implement a direct tax. In order to do this, the Federal government would have to get the people's approval. This is one of the checks and balances that the founders had implemented, due to the fear that there would one day be an out-of-control government, which would continually and forcibly impose a direct tax on the American people. The provisions that protect the people from this type of damaging behavior are in the Constitution. All you have to do is read it.

To give you a synopsis as to why the people within the Federal government are allowing this misapplication to occur, I'll explain it in simple terms. This all started years ago when the people within the Federal government had become tired of the legal requirement in obtaining the funds for their projects, in which mandated that they request, from the American people, the funds needed to implement their social programs. Most of the time the government's requests were met with high opposition by the people and; therefore, were denied. Why, you may ask? Well, to begin with, the American people did not want to pay any more taxes than they were already paying. So, when the owners of the Federal Reserve Bank, the rich foreign international bankers of the world, came to the government, in the early 1900's, they proposed a way around the Constitutional requirement that restricts the ways the government could obtain money. With greediness and laziness on

---

[33] Apportionment - apportioned -. distributed proportionately - In the context of the Constitution, apportionment means that each state gets a number appropriate to its population. For example, Representatives are apportioned among the states, with the most populous getting the greater share. Direct taxes were to be charged to the states in this manner as well.

their side, the bankers enticed our government into enacting the current unconstitutional Federal Reserve System. So, with that said, they created a cartel[34]. The parties to this cartel are the privately owned Federal Reserve Banks and that of "our" Federal government. You're probably asking yourself, why would the people within the Federal government create and enter into a cartel with the owners of the Federal Reserve Banks? There has to be a benefit right? Well, there is a benefit. The benefit is twofold. The first is that the owners of the Federal Reserve Banks are legally permitted to create "money" out of thin air, lend it out, and then charge interest for doing such. The second is that the people within the Federal government can borrow that money at will, spend it like it's going out of style, and do this all without having to go back to the American people for permission and without having to explain anything. This is illegal and flat out corrupt. Furthermore, it would be illegal for me to hold you accountable for my debt and it would be a criminal act to enforce my belief at a point of a gun. Therefore, it is a criminal act of anyone within a government entity to do the same thing, either by supporting the unlawful execution thereof or from their personal involvement in such actions. The key to understanding the truth is to recognize that the Federal Reserve Banks are nothing more than a credit card for the Federal Government or anyone of the State governments as well.

According to the Constitution there are only two ways that the Federal government is allowed to implement such a credit line. Let me put them into prospective for you. I have two scenarios for you to consider. In order to explain the first scenario lets say, for example purposes, that you have a daughter and that your daughter is getting ready to go off to college. Knowing that your daughter was about to leave for college, you ordered a credit card in her name

---

[34] A cartel is a group of companies, countries or other entities that agree to work together to influence market prices by controlling the production and sale of a particular product.

before hand. You had contacted your bank or credit card company and added your daughter to your account as an authorized user. You then gave her the credit card, that has her name on it, but upon handing the card to her you told your daughter that this card was for emergency purposes only. She agreed and went off to college. A few weeks later your daughter went out with a friend and bought an expensive dinner and dress. Question, if your daughter charges anything on the credit card is she liable for the amount charged? No, she is not. Does the bank or credit card company have legal recourse to go after your daughter if payment is not made? The answer is no. Why? She is not aware of nor did she agreed to the terms of such agreement. You were the only one that had agreed to the terms therein. Basically, she never agreed to pay back anything. You did when you signed the credit card application. On a side note, I would suggest that you think about that last statement, because an application is not an agreement. In any case, a month later you noticed that your daughter bought an expensive dinner and an expensive dress. Again, you are starting to see, month after month, that your daughter is charging a lot of items, which was never agreed upon, and in return is increasing your debt astronomically. At this point, you have three choices. First, you can call the bank and request a lower limit on the credit card. Secondly, you could call the bank and asked them to lower the interest rate so that the payments will be lower. Lastly, you can cancel her card and/or take it away. How is it that you can do any of the three? You can do so because it is your account, not hers. Your daughter does not have any authority over this account; therefore, she only has the privilege to use said account. Now, it's very important that you remember the scenario I just gave, because that is the scenario the Federal government does not want you to know. Here's the second scenario, which is illustrating the same situation; however, a twist has been added. The twist is that you are married and, unlike dealing with your child, you now have to deal with a spouse. One day you noticed that your husband or wife had applied for his or her own credit card. The next week it arrived in the mail. Over the past few months you noticed something strange, that he or she was buying a lot of junk. They in turn kept increasing their debt, which kept increasing the minimum payment on this new credit account. This is now starting to make your life miserable, because all of the available money is going to pay for this uncontrollable problem. Is it really uncontrollable? Well, you only have two options at this point. The first is to take away their credit card and close their account. But wait a second, you can't. Why? The account is in their name, not yours. So, that's not really an option is it? Just in case you are not aware, the law clearly states that the newly acquired debt automatically belongs to both spouses. Why? The law no longer recognizes you as two separate people, but rather as one person. This is all due to the marriage. Nevertheless, lets get to your second choice. You can file for a divorce in order to stop the bleeding of your wealth, but you won't do that because you love your spouse? Here's the point that I am trying to make. The Federal government would want you to believe the second, the husband and wife scenario, when it concerns government and their acquired debt. Furthermore, the government, just like with your spouse, believes that they can play the patriot card whenever they want, because you will support the government no matter how crooked they have become. Why do they believe this? They do so because they know you love your country and they have brainwashed you into believing that the government represents your country, which couldn't be further from the truth. The people, in the private sector, represent the country, not the government. Nevertheless, the truth of the matter is that our laws state that our system of government is to work like the daughter scenario, wherein you can stop the available credit and payments to the child altogether. This is what the government is afraid that you'll find out about. The Federal government is the child, the daughter that has spent uncontrollably and was assigned the authority to be a user of the credit card by the rightful owner, the parent. We the people are the parent and we are authorized to cancel the card, at any time. The Federal, State, and local governments are doing everything in their power to get the American people to believe the second scenario, not the first. We the people are the parent and, in that right, we have always had the authority to stop this overspending. Still, you may be asking yourself, then why is this happening? Well, if you don't know your rights or that you are the parent how can you then exercise your authority?

Hopefully you are asking yourself, what are the consequences of having a central bank that offers a line of credit to the governments of our country? We, as a free people, will not be able to control the governments of our country. Again, this applies to all the governments, both locally and federally. As you can see, it is happening now. What are we to do? The first is to recognize the truth as to what is occurring. Therefore, one has to remember that the governments of our country cannot repay this debt and, therefore, will be in debt to the bankers for the rest of their existence, at least if they continue with the use of Federal Reserve Notes. This is the way the system was designed. Furthermore, if the people within any one of the governments truly wanted to get out of debt they would return our country back to a sound money or currency, as the law demands. The only currency that has sound properties is that of gold and silver. For if we were to return to the use of gold and silver, as the law itself demands, there would be no principle or interest to pay back to a privately owned organization. For that reason, the American people need to wake up. The elected officials have failed us and have violated their oath to obey, uphold, and protect the Constitution of the United States of America. We, the people, are also to blame. Why? It is not our obligation nor is it our patriotic duty to pay a direct tax on our labor, especially when it is being misapplied. It is, however, our patriotic duty to resist and correct such injustices. The payment and collection of appropriate taxes are inevitable due to the purchasing of goods; therefore, it is unequivocally our duty to keep the government within the confines of the written law, the Constitution. Could it be that most of the American people have failed in their responsibilities and duties in protecting rights, liberties, and freedom because they lacked the knowledge, the intelligence, and common sense to be able to understand what is occurring? Could it also be that the majority of people do not care and, as they see it, it is more important for them to follow their favorite football team, favorite celebrity, or to know who won American Idol. Either way, this is disappointing and discouraging. This is especially true when their actions are not being hidden but are in plain sight. I'm concerned about our American liberties and the freedom that are grandparents used to enjoy. With that said, the governments of our country have started the final stage of enslaving the American people in a conceived plan to socialize America, all in the name of safety and that of the common welfare. How absurd is that? If we do not have the ability to defend ourselves or to make decisions that we feel to be appropriate for our future and safety, how can we then have any liberties, rights, or freedom? More importantly, how can we expect to be safe? The founding fathers made it clear and even warned us about having a central banking system and in doing so would be catastrophic to a free society. Nevertheless, most of the American people have ignored the warning signs. Some, on the other hand, have seen through the smoke, mirrors, and deceptions that have been implemented upon the American people. One such individual is former President Ronald Reagan. In 1982, President Reagan requested an investigation into the waste and inefficiency of the Federal government. President Ronald Reagan initiated the "Private Sector Survey on Cost Control", or "PSSCC", commonly known as "The Grace Commission". The following is an excerpt taken from the Grace commission report:

> "...100 percent of what is collected is absorbed solely by interest on the federal debt and by Federal Government contributions to transfer payments. In other words, all individual income tax revenues are gone before one nickel

is spent on the services, which taxpayers expect from their government..." Private Sector Survey on Cost Control, Report 1984

Since one hundred percent of what is collected is absorbed by the interest on the federal debt, what is the government operating on? I believe you already know the answer to this question, it's borrowed money, the corporate income tax on profits, and excise taxes like that of gasoline, alcohol, and tobacco taxes. Nonetheless, you already know as to whom the Federal government is indebted to, the Federal Reserve Banks. Some say that the United States is also indebted to China and Japan, basically other countries. I would say that this is another orchestrated scheme to take control of the American economy. Why do I say this? Well, one would have to recognize the fact that China and Japan's currency is different from ours, unless they are lending out gold and silver, which I do not believe to be the case. Outside of gold and silver or any other precious metal, China's currency is the Renminbi or Yuan, as some would say, and Japan's is the Yen. Are you seeing any yuans or yens floating around? No, you are not. Therefore, if the United States Federal government is borrowing money from these countries where are all the yens and yuans? More importantly, if the Federal government can sell securities to foreign countries in exchange for their currency why wouldn't the Federal government just have the Federal Reserve Banks print out more money in order to buy the bonds instead of selling them to foreign countries? Basically, if the Federal government can just have more money printed why is there a need for them to borrow money from another country? The reason why we, the people in the private sector, are not seeing the foreign currency floating around is because the owners of the Federal Reserve Banks have converted that currency and are in possession of such. Therefore, they have exchanged it in the form of Federal Reserve Notes. Again, if the Federal Reserve Banks can create money for the purpose of foreign currency exchange, why is it that the Federal Reserve Banks do not buy the bonds or securities offered by the U.S. government themselves? This is the question that needs to be asked.

Anyhow, the owners of these 12 regional Federal Reserve Banks are shareholders that consist of international bankers and that of international interests. They were involved in setting up the Federal Reserve in 1913. Some of the families consist of the Rockefellers, Morgan's, and Rothschild's. The Rockefeller family needs to have a lot of attention drawn to it. Why? That's because David Rockefeller, son of John D. Rockefeller Jr. and Abby Aldrich Rockefeller, had a book published in 2002 titled "Memoirs". The following is a direct quote from his book.

> *"Some even believe we are part of a secret cabal working against the best interests of the United States, characterizing my family and me as "internationalists" and of conspiring with others around the world to build a more integrated global political and economical structure — one world, if you will. If that's the charge, I stand guilty, and I'm proud of it."*

The reason why I have singled out David Rockefeller and as to what he had written in his book is twofold. The first is to prove to you that the act of treason is occurring. The second is to show the criminal mindset of this person. It takes a lot of nerve for David Rockefeller to come right out and admit what he and his family are trying to do to our country. He and everyone else, that are associated to his undertakings, should be criminally charged with treason. Lately, the actions taken by the owners of the Federal Reserve Banks, the officials within the Federal government, and that of George Soros has not been implemented in secret but rather right in the open. Moreover, in his book, David Rockefeller openly admits his criminal act of treason, but yet again the American people do nothing. If you or I had made such a claim, men with guns would have showed up at our homes, shoving us in to a vehicle, and/or into a jail cell. Still, David and his associates have resorted to flaunting their plans to undermine the American way of life. Again, this is being done not in secret but publicly. Sadly, their goals are being accomplished as we stand on the sidelines and do nothing! Due to the fact that we are not addressing or correcting the injustices it will, in my humble opinion, collapse our economy and change our way of life, as it was designed to do. The owners of the banks have always known that a catastrophic collapse was to be an inevitable result of their system. This is why the Income Tax Act was enacted at the same time as the Federal Reserve Act. More importantly, the bankers knew that one day they could get the people within the government to knowingly and willingly misapply the tax laws in order to take control of the American people. The purpose of the nonexistent personal income tax liability is not to raise revenue for the operations of government, as noted before, but to extract wealth from the American people. There are only 3 purposes for misapplying the income tax. First, it's being implemented to control inflation, which means that the bankers would have a means to extract the money that was over printed and/or created. Secondly, it's a socialistic means of redistributing the wealth of the American people. This is theft no matter how you look at it. Finally, it's an illusionary method that was implemented to make the majority of the American people a cosigner on the debt that was created by the government. This has been accomplished by misapplying the Income and Social Security Tax requirements. It has made most of the American people a slave to the government and to the bankers themselves. What could be more un-American?

Therefore, in order to restore America back to its original intent the American people need to become true tea partiers and start pouring out their tea. Mind you, that is a figure of speech.

The War On Drugs

On it's surface, it may seem like a good and respectable idea that the governments of our country have taken it upon themselves to wage a "war" on the manufacturing, distribution, and use of certain drugs, which is referred to as the "war on drugs". Over the next few minutes we are going to take a closer look at this so-called war. However, before we get started, I am going to divulge the secret that will assist you in understanding why this drug war is indeed a senseless and out-of-control idea. This is where you must use your common sense, set aside all of your emotion, and listen to your conscience. If you can accomplish this, only then will you be able to reach a logical and correct conclusion. This is very important because we are about to cover the harm that is being perpetrated primarily on nonviolent human beings. Therefore, we must recognize the fact that we are no longer living in the 18th and 19th century and that drugs are in and around our lives everyday like nicotine, alcohol, and even something as simple as aspirin. Still, don't forget about hydrocodone, OxyContin, or any of the other "legal" narcotics that are currently available. The important detail that must be acknowledged is that the drugs themselves do not harm anyone other than the person that is consuming them. This does not, in itself, justify making any drug illegal. You may be asking yourself, why do I say this? Well, what about all the legal medications that have the capability of killing someone or doing someone harm, if consumed outside of moderation or as prescribed? Should all drugs be made illegal, meaning that you will be arrested and prosecuted if you are found to be in possession of such drug? No, they should not! Furthermore, is it right for Law Enforcement Officers to have the ability to break into a person's home, late at night without identifying themselves, and by placing the occupants lives in danger, all because the occupant had decided to use a certain drug that had been deemed illegal? If not, should a raid be warranted without an investigation and conducted solely on an anonymous tip? I hope that your answer to both of those questions is no. Nevertheless, I know that the lawmakers and certain government agencies, like that of law enforcement, continue to believe that this unjust war is needed. Still, why is it that the Federal government always uses the word "war" in the title of a scheme that is unjustly being implemented upon the American people? Could it be that they have a purpose for using such a word? I believe the government is using the word for two main purposes. The first is to scare you into believing that the use of certain drugs, by another, is more dangerous to your safety than it really is. The second is to justify and to disguise the real reason behind the government's motives to incarcerate people, invade their homes, and to seize their property.

Over the years, I have discussed this issue with various types of people, both within law enforcement and in the private sector. A good portion of them have some idea that illegal drugs should remain illegal, because the drug somehow makes the user violent and they believe the user of said drug is more likely to commit a crime. However, that's not completely true. Take alcohol for example. If the consumer of alcohol is inherently a violent and disrespectful person, their use of alcohol will enhance their true nature, especially if they use it outside of moderation. When this type of person consumes alcohol, violence will pursue and their disrespect for the laws will surface. Why do I say this? They were, before the use of alcohol, inherently already a violent and disrespectful person. This is one of the reasons why bar fights occur and why an intoxicated person will get behind the wheel of an automobile. The alcohol will allow them to let their guard down, if you will. This will give their genuine disposition the opportunity to surface. In addition, no one can argue the fact that, at the point of intoxication, they will be in a mind-altering state. If, on the other hand, we are speaking about a person that is truly happy and is in no way a violent person they will, more than likely, have no issue with their consumption of alcohol. If the consumer of alcohol is experiencing personal problems it is more than likely they will become a problematic drunk. Most people turn to alcohol for the wrong reason and, more importantly, because of its mind altering effects. For some reason, they believe that the alcohol will allow them to forget their problems. However, they are not realizing that if they are thinking about their worries the alcohol will amplify their emotions to the point of an uncontrollable explosion of anger, grief, or sadness. Yet, alcohol remains legal.

If you actually believe the problem resides with the drug itself and not with the person, that had consumed the drug, you are fooling yourself. If so, you would also believe that a gun could walk into a bank, rob it, and kill someone all without a person handling it. Therefore, do you think that a spouse would ask for a divorce on the grounds that their partner was drunk when they cheated on them or on the grounds that they had committed adultery? It's upsetting to see that most people still use the effect of a substance as an excuse in order to avoid personal responsibility for their actions. It's sadder to see that other people, outside of the user, still exploit the use of the substance as an excuse to control or ruin other people's lives. You say that I am wrong? Oh, I see. Then you would believe the reason why a person would rob a bank is not because they are an immoral person, but because they had a gun strapped to their hip. Do law-abiding people, who have been issued gun-carrying permits, rob banks? Moreover, due to the fact that they are carrying guns, do Police Officers rob banks? With all sarcasm aside, can you understand how absurd that sounds?

Over a year ago, I was listening to a radio talk show where the hosts were discussing this very issue. They were also offering suggestions that could be used to put an end to this war on drugs. During this particular segment, a Law Enforcement Officer called into the show. The suggestion of ending the drug war was apparently too radical for the Officer to handle. Therefore, he called in stating, "So, when you're in a public park with your kids you wouldn't mind someone sitting next to you doing drugs like marijuana?" One of the hosts stated, "they're already in our parks and it's currently illegal." The Officer didn't even acknowledge what the host had said and continued to interrupt. The Officer continued to give nonsensical example after example without listening to any of the suggestions that were being proposed by the hosts. This event, along with others, reveals that most, not all, Law Enforcement Officers are not concerned about the unjust laws that have been created and passed, which they are blindly enforcing. This is extremely sad, especially in a free country. The point that the radio talk show host was trying to make is that marijuana, if made legal, can be banned from the public parks just like alcohol is today. Some would ask, what about the operation of a motor vehicle, while under the influence of such a drug? I would also add that, if made legal, we already have laws that address the issue of a person operating a motor vehicle under the influence of marijuana or any other drug for that matter. It's called DUI (driving under the influence). Furthermore, if it's proven that an accident had occurred due to the use of a drug, like in the case of alcohol, they should be charge with reckless endangerment. In addition, if someone was injured during the accident, the person that caused the accident should be charged with assault. Either way, this isn't rocket science. I say this for two reasons. We already have laws that deal with wrongful acts, which have caused harm to another. Therefore, there is no need for additional laws. Unfortunately, the governments of our country do not see it that way and continue to pass additional laws, but not for the purpose of making the American people safer. They are doing so to control the American people even more than what is being done today and to justify their existence. Additionally, in this situation, take allergy medication, which is a legal drug. Allergy medication is as dangerous as any other drug when it concerns a person being behind the wheel of a vehicle. In fact, there are people, all over this country, that are involved in accidents wherein the contributing factor was a person becoming drowsy after taking an allergy medication? Moreover, what should we do when a person falls asleep, while driving their vehicle, after drinking a beer or two? Here's a thought, what if the government were to pass a law that would make the manufacturing, distribution, and consumption of alcohol illegal. Oh, wait a second; they already tried that! Years ago, between the years of 1920 and 1933, the Federal government declared alcohol to be illegal and it did not accomplish the intent of stopping people from manufacturing, distributing, or consuming alcohol! If anything, it had unintended consequences. This law was referred to as Alcohol Prohibition[35]? There are only three

---

[35] Prohibition defined – *Black's Law Dictionary* – The period from 1920 to 1933, when the manufacture, transport, and sale of alcoholic beverages in the United States was forbidden by the 18th Amendment to the Constitution. The 18th Amendment WAS REPEALED by the 21st Amendment."

outcomes that will be accomplished by making a substance illegal. The first is the substance will go underground, with the criminally minded making the profits from its production. Secondly, the government agencies will get an increase in available funds in order to implement such a ridiculous ban; meaning that the innocent people will be extorted in order to pay for their operation. This is a crime in itself. Lastly, the people that had sworn an oath to protect the American people will, during the implementation of such rules, conduct multiple violations and crimes against the rights and liberties of the American people, as a whole. Here are a few of the rights and liberties that I am referring to; the right to travel, the right to privacy, and, most importantly, the right to defend ones self. Why are so many people closed-minded when it concerns the issue of legalizing drugs? There is a difference between what is right and wrong. Could it be that they don't want to see the truth because their emotions are so screwed up? Well, hopefully, this next part will assist them in opening their eyes so that they may see the truth for what it truly is.

These next statements may sound familiar and they appear to have some legitimacy; however, they are bias to say the least. Many Officers state that they feel good about themselves for taking illegal drugs off the streets. Some Officers even state that they feel good about themselves when they go into a home where there are children that don't have enough clothes or food because their parents are spending their welfare checks on drugs. This all sounds good and reasonable, but we have to be fair. This also happens to alcoholics. What's even worse is when people manufacture methamphetamine in their home and around their children. Again, don't we already have laws that address the issue of hurting and/or neglecting children? We do! Nevertheless, here's an outrageous thought. Besides the fact that drug users and alcoholics may not feed or clothe their children properly, are we, as a society, to arrest and lock up the parents of the children that are experiencing poverty? I'll let you answer that one on your own.

The biggest problem with this so-called drug war is that it is not a drug war. If anything, it is a war on the American people. To prove this, take into consideration these facts. If a Law Enforcement Officer stops a person and it is found that he or she has an illegal drug on them, even another person's legal prescription, that Officer is going to arrest that person, take their drugs; take their money, and their property. This also includes their automobile, that's if the person encountered the Officer while driving their vehicle. You tell me, how is this helping the person or even serving that person's best interest? It's simple; it's not. Therefore, how is the Officer helping the person or the community by taking them away from their family and their employment, that's to say they were employed to begin with and not on welfare? In addition, how does having an arrest record help anyone? The truth is that our government is being used to suppress the American people by turning them all into criminals and making them fearful of government, which in itself has consequences. The purpose of this type of action is to ensure that the American people are subservient when the elite bankers decide to push their one world government and to do away with the United States of America. Still, in the above scenario, which occurs on a regular basis, the law and the actions taken by the Officer have basically ruined the person's life. The sad part is that this is all due to the lawmakers passing unjust laws and that we have Law Enforcement Officers that are blindly enforcing them, without considering the consequences thereof. In return, the laws that had been passed by the government officials and the actions that have been taken by their Officers are all causing harm to the people at large. Wait a second, when a person causes harm to another, a representative of government or not, hasn't that person committed a crime? Remember, the primary element to any given crime is that there has to be an injured party. So, with that said, shouldn't the Officers and/or government officials, that had passed and implemented such a law, be punished for their actions because they were the ones that had caused the injury? Yes, they should be. Charges should always be brought forth against any person, government official or otherwise, when they have caused harm to another person. If you agree, why is that no one has been charged and punished for the passage and the implementation of the current drug laws? Oh, that's right. The people that have the authority to accept such a complaint are also part of the same government. Therefore, why would they attack their own? As long as the corrupted stay within their boundaries, their own will never betray them. It's sad to see this happening today, because it wasn't always this way. It apparently started when the title of Peace Officer had changed to Police Officer and Law Enforcement Officer. This is when most of the American public started to dislike the Police. Today, the Police, along with other agencies, have become so disruptive that their actions now border the same tactics taken by the German Gestapo. If this is how the police appear to be acting to the majority of the public, how can we then look upon them with respect? Still, it confuses me as to why the majority of Law Enforcement Officers are wondering why it is that most of the American people try to avoid them and/or why they dislike the police. Believe it or not, most of it has to do with this so-called war on drugs. This is especially true when you take into consideration that the governments of our country have arrested and/or placed on parole, probation, or put into a jail or prison cell 1 out of every 32 adults. Due to this fact, the governments of our country, which includes the Law Enforcement Officers, have nearly affected every person's life, in some way or another. I am not only referring to the people that have been arrested and incarcerated; I am referring to their friends and family members as well.

If we were to end the "War on Drugs", the Police Officer or Law Enforcement Officer would have the ability to return to the roll of a "Peace Officer", which in itself is a more respectable position. With that said, have you ever asked yourself, what happened to the role of the Peace Officer and as to why it was abandoned? I believe it was abandoned because it did not serve the interests of the socialists that have found their way into any one of our governments. Still, if we were to abolish these unjust laws, the American people would once again start to respect the roll of the Police Officer. In addition, the people will once again appreciate seeing the Peace Officer versus getting a rush of fear whenever they see a Law Enforcement Officer pull up behind them on the highway or even when such an Officer would approach someone. The ones that disagree continue to justify this unjust war on people and the illegal operations of the government by only supplying a nonsensical and emotional mindset. They do not; however, supply any facts that would support their beliefs. Therefore, as long as these injustices do not affect them, they will not care to see the truth. This, however, is not the case when they finally have been directly affected by the illegal operations of a Law Enforcement Officer. Their attitude and mindset suddenly change quickly. Still, certain Law Enforcement Officers continue to justify their criminal acts for three primary reasons. Even though most would disagree, these reasons consist of them wanting to impose their authority over others, they are addicted to their adrenalin rush, and they feel the need to justify their existence, which are all a conflict of interest when it concerns protecting the American people. As a former Law Enforcement Officer, both with the Department of Corrections and that of a Sheriff's Department, I believe I can speak as an authority on this issue. Nevertheless, it is wrong to believe that another person can punish you because you decided to exercise your liberty by choosing to consume a substance that did not result in harming another. Again, I am speaking about all drugs, not just marijuana. Remember, it's the individual that is at fault for inflicting harm upon someone else, not the drug. Oh yeah, don't forget. This also applies to the use of alcohol.

A disturbing aspect to this illegal operation is that most people state that we, as a society, need to protect the people from bad drugs. This argument is absurd. Are we to believe that no one has the right to decide which substance they want to consume or put into their own body? Let me make it perfectly clear, the ability to choose is the essence of liberty. With that said, should we then allow the government to pass a law making suicide illegal? If so, should we then charge the person that had just committed suicide with murder? Should we then allow the "authorities" to get a "No Knock Warrant" so that they can bust into the person's home, handcuff their family, throw them in jail, and seize their property? If the authorities were to do such a thing, it would be nothing more than insanity. If you agree with that statement, then answer this. What is the difference between that and the current war on drugs? There is no difference and to think otherwise would be foolish. For some of you, let me state for the record that I am not a smoker of marijuana nor am I an illegal drug user. The only drugs I am currently consuming are caffeine, nicotine, and, occasionally, some type of headache medication. Still, I believe that what the lawmakers and the Law Enforcement Officers are doing is far worse to the American people then someone using an "illegal" drug. With that said, I must reiterate that this applies to all narcotics and not just to "illegal" drugs. It doesn't matter, which one the user is influenced by, they all inhibit a person's judgment and reflexes. Still, I ask you again. Is it right or wrong to arrest and convict someone for committing a victimless crime? I hope that you are now saying, that's if you didn't already agree, that it's WRONG! As a former Law Enforcement Officer, I really liked what Barry Cooper had to say concerning this issue. Barry Cooper is a former Narcotics Law Enforcement Officer of eight years and this is what he had to say about this unjust war on people. Barry said it well when he stated, "The legal side affects of what I did caused more harm on the person and the families than the side affects of the drugs they were taking."

On average, 750,000 people a year are arrested for marijuana possession alone and now have a criminal record. Consequently, their lives are ruined. As a result, they are now having difficulty trying to obtain work and, if convicted, we will have to pay for their imprisonment. Come on, does it make any sense to ruin a person's life because they have a personal problem with a substance use? Does it make any sense that we have to pay for these individuals due to the fact that they are now in jail, even though they never actually hurt anyone? I ask you to really think about this question before you jump to an emotional answer. The problem with enforcing an unjust law may very well result in an innocent persons death. Do you recall the no knock warrants I mentioned earlier? No Knock Warrants, if you haven't heard of these types of warrants, are warrants that allow Law Enforcement Officers to enter your home without identifying themselves, without any warning, and at anytime. Before we continue, you need to take a moment and put yourself in the shoes of someone that has experienced this type of invasion. When Law Enforcement Officers are breaking into your home, without identifying themselves first, how can you decide what is or what is not a lawful invasion? Again, it really is simple; you can't! Remember, if this were to happen to you and to your family you would only have seconds to respond to the situation. So please, think about these facts before you jump to a conclusion. Better yet, try to place yourself in this situation. You suddenly hear a crash downstairs and then you hear loud voices, which you do not recognize coming towards you. What are you going to do? Your immediate instinct is to protect yourself and your family. If you have a weapon handy you are going to use it against the invaders, which had just violated the sanctity of your home. You have to agree that your chances of being shot are extremely high at this point. Again, I understand why a no knock warrant may seem to be a good practice, especially if you're a law-abiding Citizen, a lawmaker, or even a Law Enforcement Officer. However, it should never be okay that law enforcement agencies can break into our homes, seize our property, and violate our rights, all without having to show us a lawful warrant first? More importantly, why is there a need for No Knock Warrants? Can't law enforcement just wait for the individuals to leave the property? Yes, they can, but they will not get their adrenalin rush. Everyone should be concerned when damages of this magnitude occur to our families and property. As noted, there is no reason why law enforcement agencies cannot wait for these so-called criminals to come out of their homes in order to apprehend them. Matter of fact, it is safer for the Officers, the potential arrestee, pets, and family members if the arrests were to take place outside of the home. Breaking into a structure that may have potential violent people contained within it and not knowing the structural setup always poses a high risk of danger. Thus, the adrenalin rush for the Officers. Due to their unjust beliefs and their need to obtain their adrenalin fixes, Law Enforcement Officers are now raiding the homes of law-abiding Americans and, in some cases, are killing them by mistake. Don't misjudge the facts, this is happening everyday. Still think that this can't happen to you? Yes, the chances are low, but the risk still exists nonetheless. All is needed is a police informant, an unhappy neighbor, or an unhappy co-worker just to name a few.

Finally, if all drugs were made legal tomorrow most people will not become drug users for the mere fact that the drugs have become legal. Even though this is true, some say that marijuana is a gateway drug and will entice people to use a harsher drug. I, however, contend that they are referring to alcohol and not marijuana. I also argue that arresting someone, by putting them into a jail or prison cell, is a gateway to increased criminal activity within our country. Think about the implications of putting a nonviolent person in the same cell or dorm with a violent career criminal. You will successfully create another.

The War On Terrorism

Terrorism? What does this word mean? More importantly, what does it mean to you? Most of the American population is confused as to what the true meaning of terrorism is. Understanding the concept of terrorism is actually quite simple. However, in order to truly understand this concept, you must understand and recognize the aspects of terrorism. So, with that said, what does terrorism mean and what are the aspects thereof? Primarily, terrorism means the systematic use of force and violence to intimidate or coerce other people. Terrorism is nothing more than terrorizing another person or groups of people by implementing one or any combination of the aspects of terrorism. The aspects of terrorism include; threats, violence, extortion, bribery, coercion, and ultimately the use of force. The aspects of terrorism are used in order to obtain something that would otherwise be unobtainable from another person or group of people. This brings us to the next question. What is a terrorist and how do we identify such a person or persons? It is important to recognize that terrorists come in many forms and they are not limited to the people that reside in countries like Iraq, Afghanistan, or Iran. Believe it or not, terrorists are around us every day. This reminds me of a situation, that most of us can recall from our childhood, where a kid or group of kids began to bully other children at the bus stop or in their school. This may occur for a number of reasons, but let me make it perfectly clear; I am not referring to a simple fight between two or more kids. There is a huge difference between a fight over a disagreement than that of a continuing plot to harass another. On the other hand, if one or more kids continually harass another child or classmate, by plotting against them, they have successfully turned into hooligans. The reasons why this would occur can very from one kid wanting another child's lunch money to that of a youngster seeing another child as a weaker person that he or she can take advantage of. The problem with a hooligan is bigger than some may believe. The problem starts with themselves and with their self-confidence, self-esteem, or the lack thereof. Again, for most of us, we have either directly or indirectly experienced this type of behavior as a child or even as an adult. When a hooligan begins to force his or her will or behavior onto another person they have become the aggressor. Still, what do you call a group of people that continually harass and force their will onto others? Unless you're from a different world, in our society, this is what we call a gang. No matter how organized the individuals may seem to be, they are a gang nonetheless.

This also brings to mind, years ago, when organized crime was on the rise and the Mafia, along with their criminal tactics, was one of the largest gangs that had ever contributed to the high crime rate during those years. The Mafia, just like government today, would use the threat of force and destruction to extort money and property from others. The Mafia members would terrorize anyone around them, including local business owners. The Mafia's tactics were very effective due to their systematic use. These tactics include, but were not limited to; intimidation, extortion, threats, and ultimately the use of force. They were so effective in implementing their tactics that, in many ways, they had perfected the concept of "gangsterism".

Even though I have clarified the aspects of terrorism, there is one more important detail that is worth remembering. This is when these types of individuals have surfaced, by plotting their terrorizing tactics, and has caused harm to other people. In doing so, they have literally entered into the realm of terrorism. This also includes the scenario with the kids that were bullying the other children. Yes, I know. One is more of an extreme than the other, but no matter how it's perceived it is all a form of terrorism nonetheless. The point that I'm trying to clarify is that terrorism is a tactic and no one can wage a war against a tactic. That would be like waging war on war itself. Therefore, one must recognize that there are only two primary tactics that can be used to resolve any given conflict. The primary tactics include Diplomacy and War, which is the use of force. Diplomacy consists of voluntary compromise and war consists of forcing one's will upon another. Therefore, both of these have underlying tactics that can be used to gain what is sought. If you were to achieve an outcome that benefits both parties you would have had to successfully use the primary nonviolent tactic of diplomacy. If you were to obtain what you wanted through the use of force you would have had to use one or more of the underlying tactics of war, which could possibly result in retaliation from the other party. Most people would see your violent behavior as an underlying tactic of war, which could be interpreted or considered as a form of terrorism. Terrorism is as much of a tactic as the Japanese Kamikazes were during World War II, when they flew their airplanes into specific targets. Are you starting to see the truth and understand the concept of terrorism? I hope so, for the American people's sake.

None of what I am saying is by far a new concept; furthermore, Congress and the War Department both know that terrorism is an underlying tactic of war. Even though this is true, they have chosen to use the title "War On Terrorism" due to its wide assortment of aspects contained within it, as stated before. If we have officials within the Federal and local governments that do not understand this issue, we must ask ourselves this. Why are we allowing these incompetent individuals to acquire such a position of great responsibility? We do, however, have a few qualified Congressmen that actually understand the implications of this so-called War. One of them is Congressman Ron Paul, a Representative from Texas. This is what Congressman Ron Paul had to say about this very issue. "Why are we determined to follow a foreign policy of empire building and preemption, which is unbecoming of a Constitutional Republic?" ... "The catchall phrase, 'The War on Terrorism', in all honesty, has no more meaning than if one wants to wage a war against 'Criminal Gangsterism'. Terrorism is a tactic; you can't have a war against a tactic. It's deliberately vague and non-definable in order to justify and to permit perpetual war anywhere and under any circumstances. Don't forget, the Iraqis and Saddam Hussein had nothing to do with any terrorist attack against us, including that on September 11th." As you can see, we have a Congressman confirming as to what some of us have always believed about the so-called war on terrorism. First of all, the Federal government, along with Congress, knows that Saddam Hussein and the Iraqis had nothing to do with 9/11. They also knew, even though it's not mentioned above, that Saddam did NOT have any weapons of mass destruction. So again, what was the reason why the Federal government invaded Iraq? More than likely you do not have the answer to that question. Still, there are a few important questions concerning the information that the Federal government had told the American people regarding this war.

Soon after the attacks of September 11th the Federal government informed the American people that terrorists had attacked us because they didn't like our freedoms or our way of life. Do you recall this statement? I do, but not only because I heard it time and time again, but also because I found it to be the most idiotic statement that I had ever heard. Seriously, come on. Do you actually believe what the Federal government had told us about this war? I suggest that before 9/11 we, the American people, had more freedom, rights, and liberties than post 9/11. That's not to say that the Federal and local governments weren't already intruding on our liberties and freedom. At least before 9/11, the American people had the ability to conduct a peaceful protest, without the fear of incarceration. Today there are peaceful people across our country that have been attacked, beaten, and incarcerated for doing that very same thing today. There used to be a reasonable understanding, within the law enforcement departments, that when it came to the freedom of speech and the right to peacefully assemble that those rights would be upheld and respected. Post 9/11, however, has shown us that the freedom of speech is almost nonexistent and that the right to peacefully assemble is now illegal. Therefore, not only is unpopular speech no longer protected by the first amendment, it has now become an arrestable offense. The truth of the matter is that we no longer have the right to speak the truth or speak what's on our minds, at least publicly that is. We are also seeing that the government has removed the rights to personal and financial privacy, the freedom of choice, and the right to due process of Law. These are just a few of the rights that have been trampled upon since 9/11. Are we to believe that this is occurring in order to make us safer? Why would anyone allow his or her rights to be taken away from them because the Federal government had decided to wage a war on another country? We, as a country, have never allowed this to happen in the past, so why start now? Besides, who would ever suggest removing the rights, liberties, and freedom of the American people just because we are at "war"? The only people that would suggest or propose such an act would be from those who have an underlying agenda against those who possess such rights. Furthermore, we must recognize the fact; the United States has been in way more dangerous situations against other countries with more physical and technical capabilities than these so-called terrorists. We have never allowed our rights and liberties to be taken away from us in this magnitude, in time of war or otherwise. Again, does it make any sense that we should voluntarily relinquish any of our rights or liberties because of a few individuals that apparently do not like our freedom or our way of life, despite the fact that they are over 6000 miles away from us? How can this be happening, especially when we are supposedly defending the very thing that is being taking away from the American people? No one can argue the fact that our freedom and liberties are being stripped from us, but not by the Iraqis or the Taliban. It is by our own government that our rights, liberties, and freedoms are being trampled upon.

It hurts me to think, even though we have fought against more powerful enemies, that some of my fellow Americans believe that giving up their inherent rights and liberties is the solution to making us safer. If you are a person that believes in this philosophy, then you are someone who believes that we should have forbidden the Federal government from building nuclear missiles in order to counter the threat of nuclear attack from Russia, during the years of the Cold War. If I am correct, then you probably also believe that we should have more gun laws in order for us to become safer. Do you really believe that a criminally minded individual will care about the new gun laws? They apparently don't care about the law that makes armed robbery a crime. Therefore, it makes no logical sense to give up an inherent right for an illusion of safety. You and only you hold the ultimate responsibility when it concerns the protection of yourself and that of your family. If the correct solution is to take the weapons away from the American people, then why is it that the military and the law enforcement organizations across the country have the best weapons of all? At this point you must acknowledge that a new law will only affect the law-abiding peaceful people, who just want to protect themselves and their family. It will not affect the criminals from getting their hands on illegal firearms. Nevertheless, here's an analogy. Would anyone contemplate taking away your right to own and operate an automobile because of a few immoral individuals who had decided to involve their automobiles in the commission of a crime? No, that would be absurd. Wouldn't you agree? If, for some reason, you are having a hard time comprehending the logic concerning this concept, I then am afraid that you'll never understand. Nonetheless, I will not give up on our country and the founding principles in which it was created. Just because a few people had decided to commit a crime that does not mean that we can justify taking the rights and liberties away from the rest of the population. This type of thinking is nothing less than a military mindset and, in a free society, it is not warranted nor should it ever be allowed. I, however, understand the reason why the military uses this type of tactic. Despite that reason, this type of mindset should never be tolerated outside of our military nor should it be tolerated within the private sector of our Constitutional Republic. We; therefore, must acknowledge that we are giving the Federal and local governments the ability to walk all over our rights and liberties. It is even more upsetting to know that our Congress, Judges, and the American people, as a whole, have allowed these deliberate violations to occur. If no one wants to correct the injustices and to stop the deliberate violations from occurring then why in the world do we have laws to begin with?

I remember, soon after September 11th, when President George W. Bush stated that, "due to their hatred the "evildoers" have executed a plan of terror against our country." This couldn't be further from the truth. I suggest that these so-called terrorists do not hate the American people, our freedom, or our way of life; they hate the Federal government and its systematic use of force. Why did I say that, you maybe asking yourself? Well, let's think about this for a second. If China was to deploy their troops onto our street and began to kill our friends and loved ones, wouldn't you be angry with China's government? Better yet, wouldn't you be angry at the entire country of China? Don't lie! Yes, you would! One of the main reasons why you would be angry at the entire country is that the people of China allowed it to happen. As a liberty minded individual, I cannot follow the Federal government's logic. That's if you can call it any type of logic at all. If you, after everything that has been covered, still believe in and support this "War on Terrorism", then you believe that our Country can be taken down and defeated by a few mere individuals. You may not have noticed, but as the Federal government gets bigger and bigger in size it has become extremely difficult for us to protect our way of life here at home, let alone anywhere else. Therefore, ask yourself this, is the Federal government on a mission to remove most, if not all, of our rights, liberties, and freedoms in order to make the terrorist happy? If you think that I am being too radical about this issue, I would then suggest that you consider taking the time to research the Military Commissions Act and the Patriot Act, just to name a few.

If the governments, both locally and federally, have engage themselves in enacting and enforcing unjust laws that have been designed to change our way of life, by removing our rights and liberties, wouldn't those same governments be guilty of engaging themselves in terrorist acts against their own citizenry? Some would say that this does not constitute a form of terrorism. I would then have to ask, what does it constitute? Have we become so weak as a people that we have lost all courage to stand up and fight for our freedom, rights, and liberties? This appears to be true, especially when it involves "our" own government. I asked this question due to the fact that most of the American population cringes with fear when they hear a fellow American discussing a topic that concerns the Federal government or one of it's agencies. Most people, not all, have given me the impression that they are cowards when it comes to dealing with government in general. Why all the fear? Oh, I know why. The governments today will destroy you if you stand up and try to protect your freedom. The dreadful part about all of this is that this wasn't the way it used to be, but somehow it is now. The governments of our country seem to have taken the roll of the master and the people seem to have turned into being the servants. If the Federal government truly cared about our safety and that of protecting our freedom, rights, and liberties they would have not resorted to passing laws that are literally taking them away from us. We were the wealthiest, strongest, and safest country in the world not only because of our free and open economy, but because we were successful in keeping the government in check, by limiting their ability to affectively hinder the American people. Seriously, you are at more risk of being harmed from another person living within this country than that of someone thousands of miles away. This is, without any doubt, the truth. So, again, why would any true American allowed their rights and liberties to be stripped from them, especially in a time of need? This applies to not only an unwarranted traffic stop, but to the invasion of your personal financial matters. This situation reminds me of six lionesses getting ready to pounce on seventy wildebeests. The wildebeests see the lionesses and start to run away, with the lionesses in full chase. What do you think will happen if the wildebeests' were to stop then turn toward the lionesses and charge them? You guessed it. The lionesses would run away. When it concerns our rights, liberties, and freedom we need to do the same thing to the government, when they have become dangerous and out-of-control. If most of us would just reunite and turn and face the governments, both locally and federally, all of their illegal acts would stop immediately. I truly believe that the wars in Iraq, Afghanistan, on terrorism, and that of drugs would end tomorrow it the American people would just re-unite.

In ending this chapter, remember that the elected and appointed government officials are in no way smarter than you nor are they Gods. They are nothing more than human beings like everyone else. There is nothing that makes them special or all knowing individuals. They make mistakes just like everyone else. However, there is one slight difference between them and the rest of the American population. That is, they believe that they cannot be punished for their mistakes or unlawful acts. They are not above the law, even though they may believe they are. The sad part is that they are essentially immune from the Law if no one actually punishes them for their criminal acts. Today, one of the reasons why a public official may believe that he or she is above the law is due to the fact that they have either created the law or they are currently enforcing the law. This, however, does not exempt them from obeying the Law itself. If anything, you would think that they would exercise extreme care and thoughtfulness for the rights, liberties, and freedom of the American people when developing and enforcing these newly proposed and passed laws. For if they had, there would be no need of having this mindset of being above the law. The mindset that most of these public officials have is that when they knowingly pass or enforce an unjust law it doesn't matter to them, because, in their own mind, that law will never applied to them anyway.

Remember, "We hold these truths to be self-evident, that all men are created equal." With that said, everyone, including public officials, needs to adhere to the original intent of what a free America is supposed to be, where anyone can prosper and pursue the life that they had dreamed of. We, as a society, need to stop forcing our will and views onto other people, no matter where they may live. When the Federal government stops its agenda of nation building, only then will we find ourselves with no enemies. Until the time that my fellow Americans wake up and begin to understand this simple concept, only then we will begin to prosper economically, have a future for our children, and will again become a model for all the other countries to emulate.

"Sometimes it is said that man cannot be trusted with the government of himself. Can he then be trusted with the government of others? Or have we found angels in the form of kings to govern him? Let history answer this question." Thomas Jefferson

The Person That Can Change It All

Years ago, before all of the municipal and State Police Departments came into existence, everyone knew that the County Sheriffs, along with their departments, were to be the supreme law enforcers and the ultimate authority when pertaining to the protections of life, liberty, and property within the counties. Even though this is true, we must ask, are the County Sheriffs still the supreme authority and protectors within the counties? The answer may surprise you. Even though this may be unknown to most, nothing has changed when it concerns the local Sheriffs. Therefore, the County Sheriffs are still the supreme authority and protectors within the counties. Proof of this fact has always been in plain sight. In order to prove this to be true, all one has to do is take the time and look at the Sheriff's role today. If you were to take a closer look at the role of your County Sheriff you'll find that your local Sheriff is the only person that has the authority to execute warrants, property seizures, and real property evictions, just to name a few. Even though I have only identified the Sheriff, I am in no way excluding his or her deputies. The Sheriff's deputies are duly authorized to act under the authority and direction of their Sheriff. If, on the other hand, there is any doubt as to the authority of the County Sheriff, I would suggest that you conduct some research before jumping to a conclusion. In order to point you in the right direction, I would advise you to take a look at the U.S. Supreme Court case Printz v. United States 521 U.S. 898, decided June 27, 1997. This case involved two County Sheriffs, Sheriff Printz of Ravalli County Montana and Sheriff Mack of Graham County Arizona, wherein they proved that the County Sheriffs are not required to follow a federal mandate, as in a regulatory program. Not only did they prove that the County Sheriffs are not required to follow a federal law or mandate, set forth by a regulatory program, they also proved that the County Sheriffs are indeed the supreme authority within the county and are answerable to no other government, including that of the State and Federal government. This proves that the County Sheriff is the ultimate authority within the county. Therefore, if your County Sheriff is refusing to recognize this fact and/or is refusing to execute his or her oath of office then it would be the duty and obligation of the people that reside within the county to advise and mandate that their Sheriff act accordingly. If your County Sheriff will not recognize and uphold his or her oath of office it is the responsibility of the people to demand such action or replace the current Sheriff with someone who will perform as required. No matter how the situation may unfold, this will allow the proper role of the County Sheriff to once again surface and take an active part in protecting the American people. It is time that we, the American people, have a County Sheriff that will listen to the people and execute his or her office accordingly. With that said, let me explain why the County Sheriffs are the ultimate authority and protectors within their respective counties.

The reason why the County Sheriffs have been granted the ultimate authority, designated as the supreme protectors, and the final say within their counties is due to the fact that the people within the counties have delegated their authority to the County Sheriff or, in some cases, to the town Marshall. It is, for some reason, not widely known that the American people have always held the supreme lawful authority over any government. Even though the American people had delegated and empowered the County Sheriff with their authority this does not in anyway negate the fact that the American people still retain the ultimate power, as a whole. This is why the County Sheriff is an elected position, unlike the appointed chiefs of police within the municipal police departments. If you were to take a closer look, you will find that the municipal police departments have no real interest in serving or protecting the American people, even though some would disagree. Their actions speak louder than words. Furthermore, what happen to the phrase "To Serve and Protect" that used to be printed on their police cars?

Now, before we continue, let me make one thing perfectly clear. I am not stating that every Officer, municipal or otherwise, is corrupt and/or is uninterested in protecting the American people. It's sad enough that some Officers cannot distinguish the differences between a criminal and lawful act. In addition, most of the people that have found their way into the field of "law enforcement" have done so due to their low self-esteem and their search for empowerment. Therefore, they have allowed themselves to be brainwashed to the point that they no longer have the ability to conduct any critical thinking whatsoever. Along with their paramilitary training within the police academies, most of these Officers only have three concerns, outside of receiving a paycheck. Their concerns are primarily focused on obtaining and maintaining an adrenaline rush, forcing others to respect them, and their so-called brotherhood, which in itself compromises the Officer from doing what is right. This type of attitude may be acceptable in the private sector, but it should never be permitted within any government institution, let alone law enforcement. For some reason, most people believe that this does not apply to the people that have found their way into a government position. I keep asking myself, why do people believe such a thing? When an Officer displays this type of attitude he or she has, in essence, disregarded their oath and the laws of our country. It confuses me as to why some people would believe that an inherently immoral person would become moral, honest, and fair just because a badge and uniform has been issued to them.

In order to prove that the majority of these officials are guilty of violating their oath of office and have been failing in their obligations to protect the innocent, all one has to do is address the incidences that have been occurring over the past few years. When a Police Officer shoots, wounds, or kills an innocent person, by mistake or otherwise, what do you think will happen to that Officer? You're right, he or she will get a paid vacation while the so-called investigation is conducted and the chances are high that they will return to work later. In layman's terms, nothing happens to them! Most of the Officers believe that as long as they're acting within their so-called "line of duty" they are immune from punishment and that there will be no repercussions for their actions. You can prove this on your own, just look at the Officers that continually allow IRS agents to enter their cities and counties with the intent to conduct criminal behavior. This is also shown when the local authorities allow the IRS to come into their neighborhoods, conduct threatening acts of violence, and extortion practices within their jurisdiction. Furthermore, there are Officers that have taken it upon themselves to place innocent people under arrest for the mere fact of voicing their opinions, which is a direct violation of the First Amendment. One would also need to take into consideration the Officers that have gone into the wrong house, during a drug raid, and had injured or killed innocent people all in the name of justice and protecting the American people from drug dealers and/or users. This is absurd. We need protection from these types of Officers. This is where I become sick to my stomach. For if a Law Enforcement Officer or Officers were to wrongfully injure an innocent person or persons, how can they claim to be protecting the American people when they themselves are the ones that are causing the injuries and/or deaths? It, again, is quite simple, THEY

CAN'T! This is why we need our County Sheriffs to once again take their proper role within our society, which will prevent this type of insanity from impacting the innocent.

This brings me to one of two very important questions. The first, what has happened over the past fifty years that would make the American people, including the people within the law enforcement community, not to recall or understand the true nature of the County Sheriff? Well, I truly believe that it's all due to the federally subsidized educational system, which has failed the American people by not educating them on this issue among others. The Federal government, with the use of bribes, threats, and extortion efforts somehow believes that they can circumvent the ultimate authority within the counties and continue their extortion practices upon the American people. Their intent is to expand the State and Federal governments with the use of their addictive socialistic entitlements. If you cannot agree that our federally subsidized educational system has been modified and designed to dumb down the American people and to inhibit our children's critical thinking capabilities, then you yourself also lack the same ability. Therefore, we must again educate the American people on the truth concerning our County Sheriffs.

Due to the County Sheriff being an elected position, you need to recognize that the County Sheriff is the only elected protector of persons, property, and liberty within the entire country. Therefore, this is extremely important to understand. Why? The County Sheriff is our last line of defense against an out-of-control government or out-of-control people, for that matter. The County Sheriffs and their Deputies are the only rightful Peace Officers within our country. It is imperative to understand that the position of County Sheriff exists for the purpose of protecting the people and keeping the peace. This is one of the reasons why there are Sheriff Deputies within "our" courtrooms. The Deputies are to be the eyes and ears of the County Sheriffs so that no judge denies anyone of their due process rights. They are not only there to keep order within the courtroom itself, but to protect persons, property, and liberties. This was put into place by the American people, so that everyone would be ensured that the judges will remain within the Law and will never violate anyone's due process rights. If you were to take the time and research the true definition of what the County Sheriff entails you will find that the Sheriff is the Chief Executive Officer over the courts within his or her county. Therefore, it is quite simple. The Sheriffs are truly the ultimate authority and absolutely has the last say within the Counties that they reside. The sad part is, even though the majority of the County Sheriffs know this to be true, they themselves are afraid to exercise their authority. Still, some County Sheriffs today have no idea what their role should be or as to what their authorities consist of. Contrary to popular belief, the mass majority of County Sheriff's will agree with every aspect contained in this chapter. Unfortunately, if you asked them to enforce the principles of protecting their constituents against State and Federal criminals, they start backpedaling and coming up with excuses as to why they cannot help. It should make you think, is this being done on purpose? If so, could it be that ignorant people are purposely being elected so that the Federal government can vault over the restrictions within the State and Federal Constitutions, along with the protections of the County Sheriffs?

At this point, I must ask you another important question. It may come across as being silly, but bare with me. Is it okay for you and your neighbors to join together and go over to another person's home, within your community, that you may not like and steal their money or property, all at a point of a gun? I hope that you would agree that the answer is no. Still, when does this act ever become okay? I, again, hope that your answer is never. Therefore, if we are in agreement that the act of forcing someone to turn over money never becomes okay, why is it okay that the IRS can do it? Furthermore, why is it okay that the Federal government can come into the home, place of business, and bank accounts of the American people and steal their wealth, all without a court order? Well, I have a surprise for you. It's not okay! The sad part about all of this is that some County Sheriffs say that they have no authority or jurisdiction to tell federal agents to leave their county, let alone stop them from their criminal activities. That couldn't be further from the truth. Again, the County Sheriff is the supreme law enforcement authority within the county and is the chief executive officer over the courts. If you believe that a government agency has become a threat to you and to your family it is the duty of the County Sheriff to protect and defend the people from all enemies both foreign and domestic. Therefore, why is it okay for the IRS to go around threatening the American people, stealing their wealth, and basically acting like gangsters? It's because most, not all, of the County Sheriff's that have taken office, have done so without any understanding as to what their oath of office means. If your County Sheriff will not stand up and protect your person, your rights, liberties, and property then you'll need to find a Sheriff that will. It really is that simple!

Remember, two County Sheriffs brought their case before the United States Supreme Court because they felt that they were being forced into federal service without compensation, all in the manner of fulfilling a federal law called the Brady Bill. Keep in mind, that's called slavery and slavery is illegal in the United States of America. Therefore, the Court decided that the States and their political subdivisions were in no way shape or form required to follow federal direction. You see it's quite simple. No one can force another person to work for him or her, with or without compensation. These two County Sheriff's saw that the Federal government had broken the Law and they took action. They upheld their oath of office and put the Federal government back into the confines of the Constitution. The secondary reason why it was important for these Sheriffs to take their case to the U.S. Supreme Court was to prove that County and State rights and Laws supersede federal jurisdiction, which was agreed to by the Court. Therefore, in layman's terms, that means that if the Federal government wants to enter into the counties they have to go to the County Sheriff and ask for permission. If the permission is not given, they must leave! One of the justices of the court stated "...the Constitution's conferral upon Congress of not all governmental powers, but only discrete, enumerative ones." What that means is that the Federal government only has the powers that have been delegated to them within the Constitution, no more and no less. Even today the Constitution still states, "the powers not delegated to the United States [government] by the Constitution ... are reserved to the states respectively, or to the people." This is important, so pay close attention. The powers and the jurisdiction of the Federal government are few, precise, and expressly defined within the Constitution. The highest court of them all, the Supreme Court of the United States, agrees! In addition, what makes this a landmark case is that Justice Antonin Scalia went into detail explaining as to who is responsible for keeping the Federal government within their proper place. Justice Scalia stated that, if the Federal government were to go beyond its authority, the duty to protect the citizens falls upon the chief executive law enforcement officer and those of the local authorities. Therefore, one would have to conclude that the State and County governments are in charge of controlling the Federal government. Justice Antonin Scalia continued by stating, "The Federal government may neither issue directives requiring the States to address particular problems nor command the States' Officers or those of the political subdivisions [the counties], to administer or enforce a federal regulatory program. Such commands are fundamentally incompatible with our constitutional system of dual sovereignty." Take a moment and think about what you just read. While you're pondering it, let's take a look at what a regulatory program is and what sovereignty means.

Let's first look at what a regulatory program is. In order to do that, let's break it down. Common sense tells us that regulatory means to regulate by the issuance of rules, which are called regulations or laws. A program means a plan or procedure for dealing with some type of matter. Well, if all of this were true, then wouldn't Social Security be a regulatory program? Wouldn't President Obama's health care bill be a regulatory program? Isn't the Federal government's national ID card a regulatory program? There's no way around the fact that the Social Security Act and President Obama's Health Care law are both regulatory programs. Therefore, according to the United States Supreme Court, the Federal government has no authority to mandate these programs. If the Federal government has never had the authority to mandate programs of this nature one would have to conclude that all of their programs must be voluntary. Oh, that's why the Social Security Administration states that obtaining a Social Security Number is completely voluntary. It makes sense now, doesn't it? Let's now look at sovereignty[36]. Again, common sense would tell us that sovereignty means supreme authority. This definition is confirmed by blacks law dictionary as noted below in the footnote. If the United States Supreme Court recognizes each and every State as their own authority, independent of the Federal government, why do most Americans believe that the Federal law supersedes State law? Obviously, that couldn't be further from the truth. The truth is that County law supersedes State law and State law supersedes Federal law, end of story. If you take the time to read Supreme Court Justice Antonin Scalia's opinion carefully you will see that the Supreme Court recognizes two important facts. The first fact is that the Federal government cannot command the States or their subdivisions [counties] to do anything. And, secondly, it is to be recognized that the States and the Federal government are two distinct sovereigns. Therefore, we can now see the dual sovereignty that Justice Scalia spoke of.

---

[36] Sovereignty, "1. Supreme dominion, authority, or roll. 2. The supreme political authority of an independent state. 3. The state itself. *Black's Law dictionary*

In closing, everyone should know and remember that the County Sheriff, outside of a jury and jury nullification, is our last check and balance on an out-of-control government. Now that you know the pertinent information about your local Sheriff, it's time to do something with this information. Organize with your friends, family, and neighbors to spread this information far and wide. Go and interview your current Sheriff and see where his or her line is drawn. Speak with them not only as a constituent but also as a human being. The interview should be conducted in a manner that is non-threatening and as informal as possible. Remember, the purpose of the interview is to see where your County Sheriff stands and as to what he or she knows. These interviews should be handled in such a way in order to find out if they are knowledgeable of their obligations and authorities. The most important question that anyone can ask his or her County Sheriff is that will he or she stand up against tyranny. If your Sheriff is not willing to listen and he or she shows signs of being close-minded, because they think they are limited in their powers and/or abilities, get them removed from office as soon as possible. It is time to put all this weak mindedness aside and find someone that will stand up with a backbone and get the Federal government out of our lives. Our countries' principles are founded on truth, equal justice, and the freedom of choice, all of which gives you the ability to pursue what makes you happy. Hence, the pursuit of happiness that has been described and given to us in The Declaration of Independence. Always remember, if you do not have the freedom of choice then you are nothing more than a slave to the entity that has limited your choices. We need to correct this injustice by enforcing and preserving our rights and liberties, especially the freedom of choice, which is the essence of liberty.

Again, in order to preserve the rights, liberties, and freedoms that we possess, the American people need to come together and force the governments of this country to respect the people and to obey the Laws. This includes the court rulings made by the U.S.

Supreme Court that reinforces the fact that every person owns their own labor and property, which is not to be subjected to an unlawful or misapplied direct tax. This will allow the American people to once again regain their liberty, freedom, and wealth. They can start, once they have become reunited, by electing a County Sheriff that has a backbone and will stand up against this tyranny. With the help of the County Sheriff, the people should demand that property ownership, once paid off, shall be absolute and should never again be trampled upon. What I mean, when I say such a thing, is that no one should be force to put his or her property up for collateral for the purpose of securing funds for the operation of government. Everyone should stand up and stop being afraid when it concerns the interactions with a government entity. Be free by demanding your rights and invoking your liberties. Join together with your neighbors and friends. Develop discussion groups so that you and fellow Americans can understand what is happening to our beloved country. Stop living like a slave and start living like a free person. You are only free if you live like you're free. Keep in mind, slavery has been outlawed within our country; therefore, let us live our lives to reflect the same.

Remember this, most of the governmental agencies that have been created today are looking for ways to justify their own existence. This sums up all of the reasons as to why there are so many unwarranted regulations and unjust laws. If we do not stand together and address the criminal acts, which have been taken by certain governmental agencies, we will all find ourselves living in a country that we are no longer familiar with. The solution that I propose consists of the American people joining together and forcing the governments of our country to follow the law and to leave innocent people alone. It may seem like an impossible task, but as you have come to see, the County Sheriff will play a major role with assisting the American people in re-acquiring their freedom, rights, and liberties. I say this, for one very important reason. How can a system of equal justice work properly if no one in the private sector knows the truth nor do they know how the system is to operate? The answer is, it can't.

In order to bring back the original intent and purpose of what was to be our country and government, we must first restore our personal liberties and freedom. Only then will we be able to return government back to its proper role. Besides, how can we expect to resolve the unlawful actions taken by the governments of our country if we do not restore our personal liberties and freedoms first? The answer is we cannot.

America, I hope that you will wake up soon so that we can once again restart the true American dream; however, only together will we be able to accomplish this intent. Therefore, I thank you for taking the time to read what I had to say.

13983184R00127

Made in the USA
Lexington, KY
06 March 2012